FLOOD, PUNCH, BOWL BREAD, *and* GROUP SOUP

60 Multi-age Activities for Christian Kids

Lisa Flinn and Barbara Younger

Abingdon Press

FLOOD PUNCH, BOWL BREAD, and GROUP SOUP

60 Multi-age Activities for Christian Kids

ISBN-0-687-09334-1

01 02 03 04 05 06 07 08 09 10—10 9 8 7 6 5 4 3 2 1

PRINTED IN THE UNITED STATES OF AMERICA

Table of Contents

celebrating Holy Days and Holidays ...46

Sharing God's Bounty 65

Sampling foods of the Holy Land 84

Savoring Symbols of faith 101

INTRODUCTION
KIDS AND FOOD: JUST THE RIGHT RECIPE!

Have you ever noticed how attendance increases and attitudes improve when refreshments are served? We have, and we've responded by writing a book that uses food as a teaching link to the Bible and the Christian faith. Mixing the ingredients of Bible verses, historical background, prayer, and life application, we spiced them with crafts, games, songs, skits, service, outings, and a wide variety of foods from God's garden. The recipe yields one happy bunch of kids, seasoned with Scripture and warmed by the Spirit.

Cooking Suggestions:

Equivalencies: The book is created for use with nonreaders, readers, and broadly graded groups. Although addressed to churches, the activities work well for camps, day schools, home schools, and play groups.

Substitutions: Some kids are finicky eaters or have food allergies. You may want to have substitute snacks available.

Basic Ingredients: We've assumed you have these items on hand: a table, access to a stove and pot holders at church (for just a few of the activities), napkins, and paper towels. Kids love beverages, but except where specified, this is your choice.

Options: A Bible dictionary is a helpful reference for photographs, illustrations, and further information. Consider also a camera to take snapshots of your kids and perhaps a bulletin board or scrapbook for displaying the photos.

Sanitation Grade: We hope that you will lead the kids in hand-washing before food preparation. The use of pre-moistened towelettes is a quick way to clean sticky hands when you are in the middle of an activity.

May God bless you and the kids, as together you stir up fun and faith!

DEDICATION

Especially for cathy Ely:

Keep my teachings as the apple of your eye.

TASTING THE GOODNESS OF GOD'S WORD

SALT

YOU ARE THE SALT OF THE EARTH

Examine and experience this tasty mineral to understand why Jesus compares us to salt.

Matthew 5:13

You are the salt of the earth; but if salt has lost its taste, how will its saltiness be restored? It is no longer good for anything, but is thrown out and trampled under foot.

Getting Ready

Food: Loose salt; a filled salt shaker; salted and unsalted crackers

Materials: Small bowl; two baskets (optional: paper and pencil or chalkboard and chalk)

Pour two or three tablespoons of salt into the bowl. Place salted crackers in one basket and unsalted crackers in the other.

Tasting Salt

Ask: Do any of you think you will use salt today? (*Hold up the salt shaker as the kids respond.*) **Why do we use salt?** (*to make foods more tasty*)

Say: Salt flavors many of the foods we eat each day. Let's make a list of all the foods you ate yesterday. (*Each child may make a personal list with pencil and paper, or the kids may call out the foods for you to write down on the board.*)

Continue: Now let's place a check mark next to every food that

9

has some salt in it. (*Remember that even cookies and other baked goods have salt in them.*) **Now let's try a taste test. Take one cracker from each basket and take a bite of one, then the other.**

Ask: What is the difference between the crackers? (*One is salted; one is not.*) **Which one do you like the most?** (*Kids will probably choose the salted crackers.*)

Say: For thousands of years, people have enjoyed the flavor that salt gives to foods. Salt is important to us today and was considered quite valuable in Bible times. Besides flavoring soup, bread, and cheese, salt was used by the Hebrews to cure meats and to preserve olives and other vegetables. Fortunately they had a good source of salt: the Dead Sea, which has nine times more salt than regular ocean water. One way people obtained salt was by collecting salt flakes they found along the shore of the Dead Sea. At night the flakes formed on the rocks, but if they were not collected before the sun's heat shone on them, they would lose their saltiness.

Read Matthew 5:13.

Say: Of course in this passage Jesus does not mean that we are made of salt. (*Hold up the salt shaker.*) **He is saying that salt is valuable unless it loses its taste, and that we too are valuable unless we lose our faith. We must flavor our lives by loving God and showing that love to our neighbors.**

Ask: What are some of the ways we can show our faith? (*pray; help others; go to church; invite others to church*)

Say: We are going to end our activity with a Salt Ceremony. As the bowl of salt is passed, please take a pinch and put it on your tongue. When the bowl has gone all around, close your eyes for a prayer.

Let everyone taste the salt.

Pray: Lord, we are thankful for the taste of salt in your creation. Help us to be the salt of the earth by showing our Christian faith to others. Amen.

Don't be surprised if the kids now request a trek to the drinking fountain!

HONEY
PLEASANT WORDS ARE LIKE HONEYCOMB

A taste of honey and the exchange of kind words remind us of the wisdom of the proverb.

Proverbs 16:24

Pleasant words are like honeycomb, sweetness to the soul and health to the body.

Getting Ready

Food: Honeycomb; milk

Materials: Bible; plates; cups; spoons; fork; sharp knife; adhesive notepads; markers or pencils; stickers (for nonreaders)

Honeycomb can be found in some of the brands of honey available in food stores.

Separate the notepads so that every child has a section. Each section must have enough sheets to equal the number of kids.

Tasting Honey

As kids arrive, make certain to greet each one with a pleasant comment or compliment. After they are seated, using a fork, remove the honeycomb from the jar onto a plate. Slice it into small pieces and place the pieces on plates. Hand kids a plate with honeycomb and a spoon. Invite them to taste the honeycomb, explaining that they are to chew it like gum until the sweet flavor is gone. Also give each child a cup of milk to drink.

Say: **Bees must have been very busy in Bible times, because honey is mentioned from the first book of the Bible to the last. In Genesis honey is said to be one of the "choice fruits of the land"** (*Genesis 43:11*). **To the ancient Hebrews, who had no sugar, honey was their most popular sweetener. When God told Moses to lead the Hebrews out of Egypt "to a land flowing with milk and honey"** (*Exodus 3:17*), **they believed this would be a wonderful, bountiful place.**

Continue: **Honey was cultivated by beekeepers just as it is today. The bees fertilized farm crops by gathering and spreading pollen. Then they carried the pollen back to the hive, where they made honey. Beekeepers harvested this honey from the hives. Because honey was considered such a treat, the Hebrews also searched the wilderness for wild hives in the trees or rocks. Some** wilderness travelers, such as John the Baptist, actually survived on this wild honey (*Matthew 3:4*). In Bible times honey was highly valued, and people thought it was good for their health. Therefore a wise saying in the Book of Proverbs compares the goodness of kind words to honey.

Read Proverbs 16:24, then ask the kids to say it with you.

Say: Now that each of us has tasted the sweetness of honey and some of us even have sticky fingers, we are going to play a honey of a game with sticky notes. In the game we'll write kind notes to one another using pleasant words.

Give each child a marker or pencil and a portion of a notepad. Begin the game by choosing the first person to receive pleasant words. Ask the rest of the group to think of pleasant words or a compliment to write on one note sheet, then stick the sheet onto the chosen child. Nonreaders may place stickers on the child, saying a kind word as they do so. Repeat until everyone is festooned with pleasant words. Give the kids a few minutes to read the notes on themselves and others.

Conclude by leading kids in a prayer cheer:

Buzz, buzz, buzz, we're glad for bees, because they make sticky honey, buzz, buzz, buzz.

Buzz, buzz, buzz, we're glad for kind words, because they make life sweet and sunny, buzz, buzz, buzz!

May the words of the proverb sweetly stick to your kids.

GRAPES
I AM THE VINE

A wiggle game and a bit of botany help us to see that just as grapes need a vine in order to grow, we need Jesus to live fruitful lives.

John 15:5

I am the vine, you are the branches. Those who abide in me and I in them bear much fruit, because apart from me you can do nothing.

Getting Ready

Food: Seedless grapes

Materials: Bible; bowl

Wash the grapes. Separate them into serving-size clusters and place them in a bowl.

Tasting Grapes

Say: Let's play a wiggle game to help us understand how the parts of a plant work together.

Ask the kids to stand. Say: Pretend that each of you is a grape plant. Your feet are the roots. This is a how a plant gets food and water. Wiggle your roots! Your legs are the stem. The stem pulls up the food and water. Wiggle your stem! Your torso is the vine. The vine carries the food and water to the branches. Wiggle your vine! Your arms are the branches. The branches take the food and water to the leaves. Wiggle your branches! Your hands are the leaves. The leaves absorb the sunlight and carry the food and water to the flowers. Wiggle your leaves! Your fingers are the flowers that become the grapes. Wiggle your grapes!

Ask: What would happen if the branches were not connected to the vine? (*They would die.*) Why? (*The vine provides food and water from the stem and roots.*) Can a grape plant produce grapes without the vine? (*no*)

Read John 15:4-5.

Ask: What do you think Jesus is saying when he compares himself to the vine and us to the branches? (*that we cannot bear fruit without him*) Why? (*We would be cut off from our spiritual food, which is the love of Jesus.*) What kind of fruit do we bear through Jesus? (*good works; sharing of faith; living a Christian life*)

Say: Jesus asks that we "abide" in him, which means "to remain or stay" with him. If we do abide in him, he will help us grow and be fruitful.

Ask kids to bow their heads.

Pray: Lord, we ask your blessing on the fruit of the vine we are about to eat. As we taste the goodness of grapes, help us to understand that our goodness and our fruitfulness comes through Jesus. He is the vine, and we are the branches. Amen.

Serve the grapes. While the kids are snacking, explain the importance of grapes in Bible times.

Say: Grapes have been a valuable agricultural crop in the Holy Land since ancient times. The rocky hill country is a perfect place for growing large, delicious grapes. The Bible tells us of a single bunch of grapes so big that it was carried on a pole between two people! (*Numbers 13:23*)

Continue: The Hebrews planted vines in rows. They made walls from the rocks in the fields to support the vines and to catch rainfall. According to the Law of Moses grapes should not be picked from a plant until the plant is three years old. Special care was taken with all of the plants, including pruning them three times in a year. The first pruning cut away the winter damage; the second pruning cut off the non-fruiting branches; and the last pruning cut the weak fruiting branches, leaving only the strongest branches. The harvest came in the fall and was used to make juice, raisins, vinegar, wine, and jelly. Today we still enjoy all of these products.

Remember that you are an important branch to the vine of Jesus.

CHEESE
CURDLE ME LIKE CHEESE

Learn about an important Bible-times food with an energetic game and a cheese tasting.

Job 10:10
Did you not pour me out like milk and curdle me like cheese?

Getting Ready
Food: A sampling of cheeses

Materials: Bible; toothpicks; serving plate

Goat cheese and feta cheese, usually available in food stores, are similar to cheese of Bible times. Select several more common cheeses too.

Cube the cheeses and spear cubes with toothpicks. Arrange them on a plate. Those cheeses that are crumbly and cannot be cubed may be eaten with fingers.

Tasting Cheese
Begin by reading Job 10:10.
Say: Today we are going to talk about cheese.
Show the cheese platter to the kids.
Ask: What is the main ingredient in cheese? (*milk*) **Where do we get the milk to make cheese?** (*cows*) **Can the milk to make cheese come from other kinds of animals?** (*yes*)
Say: In Bible times the people mainly used goat's milk to make cheese. Goats did not need good pasture land because they like eating twigs and bark as much as they like eating grass. They provided

plentiful milk, as well as hair for weaving, meat, and leather. A shepherd with a large flock of goats was considered rich.

Continue: Sheep and goats were often mixed together and led by a shepherd to graze in one field, then another. However, dairy animals such as goats had to be milked regularly, so the shepherd could not lead them too far from the people who used the milk. Because there were no refrigerators, milk could not be stored. People needed to find ways to use the milk that they did not drink or use in cooking. Two foods made from goat's milk were butter and cheese. These could be made at home by the housewife or produced by a cheesemaker. Cheese stored and traveled well and made a tasty addition to the Hebrew diet.

Tell the kids that in celebration of the ancient history of cheese, they will now play an old game with a new name, the Shepherd in the Field. This is a biblical version of the Farmer in the Dell.

Here's how to play the game: Arrange kids in a wide circle. Choose a player to be the shepherd. Lead the kids in singing the first verse. During the second verse the shepherd walks around the circle and chooses a wife, then goes to the center of the circle. During the next verse the wife chooses a child, then goes to join the shepherd. This continues until everyone is in the center. The song then calls each player, one by one, to leave the center until everyone is back in the circle, except the "cheese."

Lead the song as kids sing along. You may need to add or delete verses to suit the size of your group. (If the group is quite large, have the goat take several kids.) Make certain, however, that the last verse with the cheese is used.

Sing:

The shepherd in the field, the shepherd in the field,
Hi ho the dairy-o, the shepherd in the field.

The shepherd takes a wife, the shepherd takes a wife,
Hi ho the dairy-o, the shepherd takes a wife.

The wife takes a child . . .
The child takes a sister . . .
The sister takes a brother . . .
The brother takes a dog . . .
The dog takes a goat . . .
The goat takes a kid . . .
The kid takes a cat . . .
The cat takes a mouse . . .
The mouse takes the cheese . . .

Then sing to return players to the outer circle:

The shepherd goes back home, the shepherd goes back home,
Hi ho the dairy-o, the shepherd goes back home.

The shepherd takes a wife, the shepherd takes a wife,
Hi ho the dairy-o, the shepherd takes a wife.

The wife takes a child . . .
The child takes a sister . . .
The sister takes a brother . . .
The brother takes a dog . . .
The dog takes a goat . . .
The goat takes a kid . . .
The kid takes a cat . . .
The cat takes a mouse . . .
The cheese stands alone . . .

Invite the "cheese" to be the first seated for the sampling of cheeses.

Pray: Thank you, Lord, for songs and games, friends and family, milk and cheese. Amen.

Serve the cheese platter, identifying the types of cheese for the kids.

WATER
A CUP OF COLD WATER

Relay runners rush to welcome others in the name of a disciple, emphasizing Jesus' wish for us to welcome believers.

Matthew 10:42

And whoever gives even a cup of cold water to one of these little ones in the name of a disciple—truly I tell you, none of these will lose their reward.

Getting Ready

Food: Water

Materials: Bible; bathroom-sized paper cups; masking tape; two non-breakable water pitchers; nametags; markers

Decide where you will hold the relay race, either outdoors or in the fellowship hall or church gymnasium.

To prepare for the relay, set up a table at the starting point. Determine how far the relay will be run, based on the age of your kids. Mark the finish line by laying down a strip of tape parallel with the table. Next, put out a stack of cups and a pitcher of water at each end of the table.

Tasting Water

Ask: **Where do we get our drinking water?** (*wells; city water plant; rivers; reservoirs*) **Does our area ever have a water shortage? If so, why?** (*lack of rainfall; dry season*)

Say: **There are places in the world, such as the Holy Land, that experience a dry season. In Israel there is little rainfall from April until October. Then when the rainy season begins, it rains often, through the month of March. When people live in a land that has six months of rain and six months without, they must be prepared. To save rainwater, many Hebrews built cisterns or water tanks. They did not have water faucets in their houses. If they needed water, they had to carry a jug to the well, to a spring, or to the cistern. Each and every day people fetched all of the water they needed for cooking, drinking, cleaning, and bathing.**

Continue: **Since they had to work hard to get it, the Hebrews appreciated water. It was considered a kindness for those drawing water at the village well to offer a drink to passing travelers. And when someone knocked on the front door, a good host or hostess offered a cup of cold water to a friend or a stranger.**

Continue: **In the Bible Jesus sends his disciples into the countryside to help people. He speaks about this cup of cold water.**

Read Matthew 10:40-42.

Say: **To help us remember to welcome people into our church and into our homes, we're going to run the Cup of Cold Water Relay.**

To prepare for the race, slowly read the names of the disciples listed in Matthew 10:1-4, telling kids to listen carefully. Then give them nametags, asking them to write a disciple's name on the tag. Put the tag on their shirts. Assist nonreaders in selecting a name and writing it on the nametag.

Next, divide everyone into two teams. The first runners from each team will stand at opposite ends of the table. Line up the remaining team members in single file, opposite from their first runner, just behind the masking tape finish line.

Explain the game: When you say "go," the first runners will fill a water cup halfway with water, race to their teammates, and **say: "Welcome in the name of** (*the name on their own nametag*). The first person standing at the masking tape finish line will drink the water;

dash to the table; pour a cup of water; then run back to the finish line, **saying to the next person: "Welcome in the name of** (*the name on their own nametag*)." Meanwhile, the first runner will go to the end of the team's line. The race continues until each person on each team has been welcomed with water. The runners who began the relay will drink the last cup. Toast the winning team with cups of water!

Pray: Lord, thank you for the wonderful water we enjoy: from ice cubes, swimming pools, and fancy bottled water to hot baths, clean dishes, and garden sprinklers. We thank you for your Son, Jesus, and his wise teachings. May we remember that we can serve you, even by sharing a cup of cold water. Amen.

Now help yourself to a glass!

BREAD
THE BREAKING OF BREAD

Come to understand what it means to break bread together by offering grace, sharing a loaf, and singing a spiritual.

Acts 2:42
They devoted themselves to the apostles' teaching and fellowship, and to the breaking of bread and the prayers.

Getting Ready
Food: A loaf of unsliced bread

Materials: Basket; tea towel or napkin; plain paper placemats or white paper; crayons

Wrap one end of the loaf with the towel, then place it in the basket. Put the basket in the center of the table. At each child's place lay down a placemat or a sheet of paper, along with crayons.

Tasting Bread
Begin by asking kids to decorate their placemat in preparation for the snack. Suggest that they draw the bread in the basket or that they print out their favorite table grace with fancy lettering.

When the group is nearly finished, ask volunteers to recite the table grace they say at home or to sing a grace learned at camp or at vacation church school. Afterwards, thank those who shared, then ask the kids to bow their heads as you say your favorite table grace.

Ask: Has anyone ever heard or read the expression "the breaking of bread?" Any ideas about what it means? (*to break off a piece of bread; to eat together*)

Say: Today we are gong to break bread together. To do this, one person will hold the bread on the towel end while the person on the right breaks off a piece. I will start by holding the loaf, and we'll pass it around the table.

Tell kids to hold their piece of bread until everyone has been served. Let the kids eat the bread.

Say: After the death and Resurrection of Jesus, the first Christians gathered together for lessons taught by the apostles and for prayer. They often met in one another's homes, where they enjoyed meals and one another's company.

Read Acts 2:42.

Say: In Bible times people broke off pieces of bread from the loaf to eat, just as you have done today. Over time the words *breaking bread* **came to also mean "sharing a meal." I'm glad we could break bread together and enjoy one another's company today.**

Send the loaf of bread around the table again. Conclude with the singing of the first verse of "Let Us Break Bread Together." (This hymn can be found in many hymnals.) Explain that the hymn is a spiritual, a song written by African-American Christians many years ago, and is based on the verse they just heard, Acts 2:42. You may want to ask kids to get on their knees to sing:

> Let us break bread together on our knees,
> Let us break bread together on our knees,
> When I fall on my knees with my face
>   to the rising sun,
> O Lord, have mercy on me.

African-American spiritual; Acts 2:42; adapted and arranged © 1989 The United Methodist Publishing House.

And while you are on your knees, see any crumbs?

FRUIT
BEAR GOOD FRUIT

A Good Fruit Collage and a sampling of fruit reinforces our understanding that good people bring forth good works.

Matthew 7:16-17

You will know them by their fruits. Are grapes gathered from thorns, or figs from thistles? In the same way, every good tree bears good fruit, but the bad tree bears bad fruit.

Getting Ready

Food: A sampling of fruits

Materials: Bible; serving plate; toothpicks; posterboard; markers; old magazines; scissors; glue

Prepare the snack by washing or peeling the fruit, then slicing it into bite-sized pieces. Spear with toothpicks and arrange on the plate.

On the posterboard draw an outline of a tree. Around the treetop draw a variety of fruits: apple, peach, banana, pear, lemon, orange, and so forth. On the stem of each fruit write one of the children's names. You can wait until kids arrive to do this if you are unsure who will be there.

Tasting Fruit

Begin by serving the fruit sampler. As the kids taste the variety of fruits, work together to identify each fruit. As you do so, have the kids name the tree that bears each type of fruit (banana tree; apple tree).

Ask: Can we harvest any of these fruits from a thorn tree? (*no*) **What grows on a thorn tree?** (*thorns*)

Read the words of Jesus from Matthew 7:16-17.

Say: When Jesus says, "You shall know them by their fruits," he is talking about trees, and he is also talking about people. Good trees grow good fruit. Good people do good deeds. I know you have many ways of showing goodness to others. Think of a kind, happy, helpful, or creative way that you can show goodness, then write it on the piece of fruit that has your name. (*Example: I smile at everyone; I help feed the dog.*) **Assist nonreaders.**

When everyone's good work has been recorded on the poster, bring out old magazines, scissors, and glue. Challenge the group to find lots of pictures of fruit and fruit products to glue on the poster's tree. Tell them they are going to grow a really goofy fruit tree. Laugh with the kids at the fruit tree they are creating.

Pray: **Thank you, God, for good fruit from good trees, and for good deeds from good people, and for good fun with good friends. In Jesus' name we pray. Amen.**

Thanks to you for your good deed of teaching!

COLD AND HOT
I WISH YOU WERE EITHER COLD OR HOT

A fun taste test leads us to realize that Jesus does not like lukewarm faith.

Revelations 3:15-16

I know your works; you are neither cold nor hot. I wish that you were either cold or hot. So, because you are lukewarm and neither cold nor hot, I am about to spit you out of my mouth.

Getting Ready

Food: Hot cocoa mix; chocolate milk; chocolate ice cream; water

Materials: Bible; saucepan; bowls; mugs or hot cups; spoons; ice cream scoop; pot; ladle

Before kids arrive, take the chill from the chocolate milk by warming it slightly in the saucepan. When it feels lukewarm, pour it back into the container. Next, heat water and prepare the cocoa mix according to the package directions.

Tasting Hot and Cold

Begin by serving a half cup of hot cocoa to each child. Take care with younger children, reminding them that the cocoa can burn them.

Ask: **What is your favorite time to drink hot cocoa?** (*fall; winter*) **Does drinking hot cocoa warm you up or cool you down?** (*warms you up*) **Are there special times when you like to drink hot cocoa?** (*skating parties; after hayrides*) **What is your favorite time of year for ice cream?** (*spring; summer*)

Next, serve kids a scoop of chocolate ice cream.

Ask: Does eating ice cream warm you up or cool you down? (*cools you down*) **Are there special times when you like to eat ice cream?** (*birthday parties; outings to the park*)

Now, pour kids a half cup of the lukewarm chocolate milk.

Ask: Do you have a favorite time of the year for drinking lukewarm chocolate milk? Does it warm you up or cool you down? (*neither*)

Continue: Everything we have tasted today is chocolate-flavored, but how are they different? (*temperature*) **Which did you like best?** (*Kids will probably answer cocoa or ice cream, not the milk.*)

Read Revelations 3:15-16.

Explain to the kids that Jesus was unhappy with people's wishy-washy behavior and lukewarm service to others. These people left a bad taste in his mouth because they did not have a strong faith.

Say: We don't want to be lukewarm like those people. We want to have a strong faith and show it.

Ask: What are some ways we can show our strong faith? (*come to church; help others; pray every day; take time to listen to or read Bible stories; tell others about our Christian faith*)

Pray: Dear God, we want to be strong in faith, and we want to show our faith by the way we act. We pray that we will not be lukewarm in our love for you. Amen.

Kids may enjoy second servings of the chocolate foods.

Go ahead, indulge yourself too.

MUSTARD
THE KINGDOM OF GOD

Tasting mustard and illustrating the parable of the mustard seed on a cookbook marker helps us begin to understand the kingdom of God.

Mark 4:31

It is like a mustard seed, which, when sown upon the ground, is the smallest of all the seeds on earth.

Getting Ready

Food: A sweet mustard dip or salad dressing; hot dogs; mustard seeds

Materials: Bible; bowls; toothpicks; knife; index cards; clear self-adhesive paper; crayons; scissors; glue.

Pour dip or dressing into several bowls. Cook hot dogs and slice them into bite-sized pieces, placing them in bowls too. Vegetarian hot dogs are available in the freezer section of most food stores if you want to offer them as well.

Tasting Mustard

Begin by placing a single mustard seed in the palm of your hand, then showing it to the kids. Ask them to speculate as to how big a plant might grow from the seed.

Say: **This is a yellow mustard seed, which is the most common type of mustard used in cooking today. The yellow mustard grows to be about eighteen inches tall. However, the mustard in Bible times grew from a tiny black seed into a giant bush. Jesus thought mustard was such an amazing plant that he used it in a story.**

Read Mark 4:30-32.

Say: **The Hebrew people saw this plant all the time along the roadside and in the fields Jesus hoped that if the people could appreciate the miracle of such a small seed becoming a huge shrub, then they might believe in the wonder of God's kingdom.**

Ask: **What do you think Jesus means by God's kingdom?** (*the whole universe; everything in heaven and on earth; the entire natural and spiritual world*)

Say: **Even though we may only see or understand the tiniest bit of it, God's kingdom is surprisingly big. It is bigger than we can imagine and has room for all of us.**

Next, lead the kids in an action prayer. Have them kneel, with head to knees and arms tucked over head.

Pray: From a tiny mustard seed, a giant bush will grow. (*Stand and reach arms high.*) **God's kingdom reaches everywhere.** (*Twirl around while swaying arms.*) **This I truly know.** (*Put hands over heart.*) **Amen.**

You may want to repeat the prayer a time or two.

Serve the snack.

Ask fun questions: What is your favorite food to eat with mustard? Has anyone ever eaten hot mustard? Has anyone tasted spicy mustard greens?

Next, bring out the index cards and crayons. Invite kids to draw a giant mustard bush, possibly filled with colorful birds. Explain that their pictures will become cookbook markers for them to keep or give as a present.

When kids are finished, ask them to sign the backs of their cards. Next, they are to use a drop of glue to affix mustard seeds to their drawings.

To cover with clear self-adhesive paper, place cards side by side on the sticky surface of a length of the paper, with edges touching. Complete by folding the cards over against more of the sticky surface. Using scissors, cut the cards apart and trim edges, if necessary. Spread the cookbook markers out for all to admire.

Keep that mustard seed faith!

A TASTE OF THE WORLD
DISCIPLES of ALL NATIONS

While pretending to be guests at an international Christian conference, visit four booths to learn about different churches and to sample international foods.

Matthew 28:19

Go therefore and make disciples of all nations, baptizing them in the name of the Father and of the Son and of the Holy Spirit.

Getting Ready

Food: Rye or dark bread; cream cheese spread; cooked chicken nuggets; garlic butter; red or black pepper; oranges; fresh or canned coconut milk; Danish butter cookies

Materials: Bible; serving plates; bowls; cups; knives; 24-inch lengths of yarn; index cards; stapler; markers; tape; posterboard or craft paper; (optional: photocopies or hand-drawn flags of Russia, Ethiopia, Brazil, and Denmark)

Kids will visit four booths created for the four countries they will pretend to visit. Set up the activity so that kids will either walk around a room with four separate tables or walk around one table divided into four areas. Create the booths by printing the name of each country—Russia, Ethiopia, Brazil, and Denmark—on posterboard or craft paper. Decorate with flags, if you have them. Hang these signs with tape on the table front or on the wall behind.

Arrange the following foods and place them at the appropriate booths:

Russia: Sliced bread and cream cheese spread. Set out knives.

Ethiopia: Cooked chicken nuggets and warmed garlic butter seasoned with pepper.

Brazil: Orange slices and coconut milk. Pour a small amount of coconut milk into each cup.

Denmark: Butter cookies.

Finish the preparations by laying out the lengths of yarn, index cards, markers, and stapler. Have the kids make nametags that say: "Hello, my name is . . ." To help younger kids or to save time, you may want to tie the ends of the yarn to create a loop, then staple the knot to the index card ahead of time.

Tasting a Bit of the World

Begin by asking kids to make nametags and to place them around their necks. As they put them on, greet the kids by name, shake their hands, and introduce yourself as their tour guide.

Say: Welcome to the International Conference of Christians. As your guide I will take you to four different booths to hear some facts about the Christian church in each country and to taste some of their traditional foods.

Read Matthew 28:19. Explain that Jesus told his disciples to "go therefore and make disciples of all nations" and that over the centuries, the Christian church has spread throughout the world.

Say: As Christians we all pray to God and read the Bible, but we do so in our own languages. We all take Holy Communion but we may use different types of cups and kinds of bread. Each of our countries has its own favorite foods to serve at a potluck or a picnic, and each has its own special church traditions. The conference is beginning. Let's go!

Lead the group to Russia's booth.

Say: This country's Christians are mostly Russian Orthodox. Some of the fancier church buildings are topped with onion-shaped domes. Inside these churches are painted images, which we call "icons," of Jesus and the disciples. On Easter Sunday the priests walk around the church three times, then knock on the door asking for the body of Christ. The congregation inside the church calls out, "He is not here. He has risen!"

Invite the kids to sample the bread with cream cheese, then lead them to Ethiopia's booth.

Say: Almost half of Ethiopia's population is Christian. The typical church building is round and made of stones or stucco. Inside, where people worship, there are paintings of Jesus, Mary the mother of Jesus, other Bible people, and angels.

Ask kids to taste the chicken dipped in garlic butter. When they are finished, proceed to the Brazilian booth.

Say: Brazil's population is primarily Roman Catholic. In larger cities the churches may be grand in both size and decorations. Many have real gold trim and life-sized statues of Bible people. In church worshipers greet one another by saying, "Paz de Christo" and shaking hands.

Encourage the kids to taste the coconut milk and the orange slices. Finally, take them to Denmark's booth.

Say: There are many Lutheran churches in Denmark. One church that is quite old was originally built in the shape of a ship. This seafaring country likes the Christian symbol of the ship and many churches have a model of a ship hanging over the center aisle.

Invite kids to enjoy the butter cookies.

Pray: God of all people, we give thanks that we are part of a Christian family that stretches across the world. Help us all to be good disciples of Jesus, no matter where we live. Amen.

Thank kids for coming to the International Conference of Christians and encourage them to visit the booths again for a taste of this or that.

Via con Dios!

EXPLORING STORIES OF THE OLD AND NEW TESTAMENTS

THE CREATION
EVENING AND MORNING COOKIES

Decorated cookies provide a tasty incentive for listening carefully to the first story in the Bible.

Genesis 1:5

God called the light Day, and the darkness he called Night. And there was evening and there was morning, the first day.

Getting Ready

Food: Sugar cookies; one can chocolate frosting; one can vanilla frosting; several tubes of yellow frosting

Materials: Bible; knives; pencil; paper

Each child will need two cookies, one for decorating as morning and one for decorating as evening. Be sure to have extra cookies in case some crumble.

Exploring the Story of Creation

Begin by inviting kids to take the Evening and Morning Quiz. Explain that they are to answer either "evening" or "morning" to your questions.

Ask: When does the alarm clock ring? (*morning*) **When do the street lights come on?** (*evening*) **When does Sunday school meet?** (*morning*) **When does the sun rise?** (*morning*) **When do**

we eat supper? (*evening*) When do we go to school? (*morning*) When do we say our bedtime prayers? (*evening*) When do we go to the Christmas Eve service? (*evening*) When do we go to the Easter sunrise service? (*morning*) And here's a trick question: When should we brush our teeth? (*morning and evening*)

Say: **I see you have a good understanding of evening and morning. That's great! You're ready to hear the story of how God created the world, but first we'll decorate Evening and Morning Cookies.**

Show kids the decorating supplies and give each person two cookies. Explain that one cookie is to be frosted in chocolate and dotted with yellow stars, while the other cookie is to be frosted in vanilla and decorated with a yellow sun. Tell kids not to eat their cookies yet, as they will use their creations during the story.

When the kids are finished frosting, explain that as you read the story, they are to hold one cookie in each hand. Say: **I'm going to read to you from the very first chapter of the very first book of the Bible. This is the Book of Genesis. The Creation story has lovely, poetic language. If you listen carefully, you will hear the phrase, "There was evening and there was morning" repeated six times. Every time you hear me say, "There was evening and there was morning," take a nibble from your Evening and Morning Cookies.**

Read Genesis 1:1—2:2.

Then invite the kids to express their favorite parts of God's creation as they finish their cookies. As kids speak, make a written note of what each child says for use in the closing prayer.

Pray: **Bowing our heads to you, our heavenly Maker, we offer thanksgiving for the beauty of day and night, earth and sky and sea. We praise you for flowers and fruit, birds and bees, animals and people, fish and sea monsters, and vegetables and trees. Each of us says a special thanks too.** (*Child's name*) likes (*favorite part of creation*). Continue by saying each child's favorite part of creation.

Conclude: **You have surrounded us and amazed us with the wonder of your creation. Thank you for this world, which is our home. Amen.**

May God bless you when morning has broken and all through the night.

NOAH'S ARK
fLOOD PUNCH

Mixing Flood Punch and pantomiming ark animals creates a lively celebration of God's rainbow covenant with us.

Genesis 7:15

They went into the ark with Noah, two and two of all flesh in which there was the breath of life.

Getting Ready

Food: Animal crackers; Flood Punch

Materials: Bible or Noah's ark picture book; serving bowl; punch bowl; ladle; cups

Recipe for Flood Punch: One two-liter bottle of lemon-lime soda; one 46-ounce can of pineapple juice; one 12-ounce can of frozen concentrate lemonade; one cup water; 10 or more drops of blue food coloring.

Chill ingredients. Combine in a punch bowl. Add more food coloring, if desired. Yields 25 five-ounce servings.

Have the ingredients for the snack and the serving pieces at hand. When the time comes, kids will help prepare and set out the snack.

Exploring the Story of Noah's Ark

Begin by reading the story of Noah and the Flood, either from a picture book or from the Bible (Genesis 6:13—8:12 and 9:13-15.)

Ask: Why did God send a flood? (*Because people were behaving violently.*) **Who and what was on the ark?** (*Noah and his wife; his sons and their wives; two of each kind of creature; and every kind of food*) **How long did it rain?** (*forty days and forty nights*) **What sign did God send to show there would never again be a worldwide flood?** (*a rainbow*) **Do you know what a covenant is?** (*A covenant is an agreement between two or more people or groups.*)

Say: God promised never to destroy the whole earth again with a flood. That is God's part of the covenant. Our part of the covenant is to behave like Noah. God wants us to be good, fair, and faithful even if we live in a violent world. When you see a rainbow in the clouds or in a picture, think of Noah and the flood. Remember your part of the covenant is to be good, fair, and faithful.

Next, have the kids help you combine the punch ingredients and put the cookies into the bowl. As you serve the animal crackers and Flood Punch, ask the kids to think of an animal who was saved by Noah's ark.

When the snack is finished, ask for a volunteer to be the leader and to imitate or pantomime one of the animals. After the group guesses the animal, everyone will follow the leader and pretend to be that animal too. Play until all who wish to have had a turn to be the leader.

Conclude with the following prayer. After you state each phrase, have the kids repeat it.

Pray: Dear God, thank you for rain and rainbows . . . for animals and the ark . . . and for Noah and your promise. Amen.

It's time to clean up. Sure beats mopping up the ark!

MOSES IN THE WILDERNESS
GATHERING MANNA

A trek through the wilderness and a search for manna make us mindful of God's steadfast love and care.

Exodus 16:31

The house of Israel called it manna; it was like coriander seed, white, and the taste of it was like wafers made with honey.

Getting Ready

Food: Miracle Manna

Recipe for Miracle Manna: Serves ten kids for this activity. One package filo dough, unthawed; ⅓ stick butter; ⅓ cup honey or corn syrup; 3 tablespoons sugar; nonstick cooking spray (optional: 1 teaspoon ground coriander)

Filo dough may be found with frozen pie crusts in the freezer case. This recipe is based on 9-by-14-inch pastry leaves (package contains 40 leaves), but varying sizes of filo dough will work.

Preheat oven to 400 degrees. Melt butter with honey or syrup. Stir in sugar and optional coriander.

To begin the layering process coat a baking sheet with nonstick spray and place one filo leaf on the sheet. Work quickly before the leaves dry out. Brush with the butter mixture, then place another filo leaf on top. Repeat until eight layers have been brushed.

Bake in the oven for five minutes or until golden and just browning on the edges. Remove from the oven and immediately cut into pieces (four pieces per child.) If you expect a group larger than ten, make more batches of manna.

Materials: Bible; sandwich bags; pastry brush; knife (optional: water fountain)

Prepare the Miracle Manna ahead of time. Bag each piece of manna into a separate sandwich bag.

Before the activity begins, scatter the bagged manna in three locations: one bag per child at the starting point; one bag per child at the midpoint; and two bags per child at the finishing point. When you lead kids through the desert in search of manna, to be Biblically correct, each bag will be referred to as an "oner" of manna.

Exploring the Story of Manna

Ask: **Does anyone remember why Moses and the Israelites were wandering in the wilderness?** (*They were fleeing slavery in Egypt and going to the Promised Land.*) **How long were they walking in the wilderness?** (*forty years*) **Do you suppose they needed a source of food on this long journey?** (*yes*)

Say: **Yes, they desperately needed food. They began to worry so they complained to Moses. As we hear their story, we will pretend to be the Israelites gathering food in the wilderness.**

Read Exodus 16:12-16. Ask the hungry travelers to each gather one oner of manna and then be seated.

Next, read Exodus 16:17-19 as they enjoy their manna.

Lead the wanderers to the second stop. Read Exodus 16:20-21. Let kids each find one oner of manna. This time, after they have eaten, you may want to walk by a spring of water (fountain) on the way to the final stop.

Read Exodus 16:22-23. Instruct the wayfarers to take up two oners apiece this time. Tell them that they may eat only one as they listen to Exodus 16: 24-26. Next, the good observers of the Sabbath may nibble on their last bit of manna as they rest and hear Exodus 16: 31-35.

Say: **God provided for the Israelites' escape from Egypt, for the crossing of the Red Sea, for the guiding clouds of pillar and fire, and for food in the wilderness until they arrived at the Promised Land. God provides for us too. The Israelites lifted up** their needs to God, just as we do when we pray. What we truly need may not be the same as what we want. Prayers are answered in God's way, which is sometimes mysterious to us.

Continue: Manna is still a mystery that has puzzled scholars for ages. The Israelites didn't know what it was, either. The word *manna* may have come from the Hebrew word meaning, "What is it?" or from the Egyptian word for food. Some think the word might have come from the combination of the Hebrew and Egyptian words to mean, "Is it food?" One thing we know for sure is that manna was food and that God provided, for the Israelites just as God provides for us.

Pray: Lord, we pray that you will guide us and provide for us just as you did when you sent manna long ago. Amen.

Thanks be to God for the manna in our lives.

THE BIRTH OF JESUS
MANGER HAYSTACKS

Hearing the Bible story, making Manger Haystacks, and singing about Jesus asleep on the hay reminds us of our Savior's humble birth.

Luke 2:7
And she gave birth to her firstborn son and wrapped him in bands of cloth, and laid him in a manger, because there was no place for them in the inn.

Getting Ready
Food: Manger Haystacks

Recipe for Manger Haystacks: One 11-ounce bag of butterscotch morsels; one 5 ounce can chow mein noodles; nonstick cooking spray (optional: 1 to 1½ cups peanuts)

With non-stick spray, lightly coat the inside of a microwave-safe bowl, about 2½ quart size. Pour morsels into bowl, cover loosely with plastic wrap, and heat on high for 2½ minutes. Pour noodles and optional peanuts into the morsels and mix with a fork until the noodles are thoroughly coated. (If you don't have a microwave, melt the morsels in a double boiler or in a saucepan, stirring constantly.)

Coat two baking sheets with nonstick spray and immediately have kids drop the mixture by spoonfuls onto the sheets. These drop cookies usually set up within twenty minutes. To speed the process you may want to slide the baking sheets into the refrigerator for five to seven minutes. Yields three to four dozen cookies, depending on the use of peanuts and serving sizes.

Materials: Bible or picture book about the birth of Jesus; mixing bowl; large spoon; spoons; baking sheets; plates; plastic wrap (optional: hymnals)

Kids will make the Manger Haystacks as part of the activity.

Exploring the Story of Jesus' Birth

If you have hymnals, hand them out, giving kids the hymn number for "Away in a Manger." Otherwise, just repeat each verse for the kids before you lead them in singing. **Say: Now we're going to sing the first verse of a beloved Christmas carol, "Away in a Manger":**

Sing:
Away in a manger, no crib for a bed,
The little Lord Jesus laid down his sweet head.
The stars in the sky looked down where he lay,
The little Lord Jesus, asleep on the hay.

Ask: If Jesus had no crib for a bed, where was he sleeping? (in a manger) **What is a manger?** (a feed trough, usually made of wood) **What was used to make the manger soft for Jesus?** (hay)

Now sing the second verse of the carol:

The cattle are lowing, the baby awakes,
but little Lord Jesus, no crying he makes;
I love thee, Lord Jesus, look down from the sky
and stay by my cradle till morning is nigh.

Anonymous; based on Luke 2:7.

Ask: In what kind of place was Jesus born? (barn or stable) **Why do we think this?** (Cattle are mentioned; the Bible tells us.) **Was Jesus unhappy in his manger bed?** (no) **How do we know?** (The song says he doesn't cry.)

Say: Even though Jesus was a very special baby, his birth did not take place in a royal palace, a fine home, or a fancy inn for travelers. Jesus was born to ordinary people who could not find a room in which to stay. His humble birth in a stable was one

way that God showed us that he sent Jesus to love, teach, and care for ordinary people like you and me.

Next, invite the kids to make Manger Haystacks.

While the haystacks set up, read Luke 2:1-26 from the Bible or the picture book.

After the reading, have the kids stand in a circle, asking them to join hands for prayer. Start the prayer by having each person say in turn, "Thank you."

Pray: Thank you, God, and hooray for your Son, who slept on the hay. Amen.

Enjoy the handmade treats and another round of "Away in a Manger."

Bless newborn babies everywhere!

JESUS LEARNS AT THE TEMPLE
LUNCH BOX FOODS

Just as Jesus questioned his teachers, kids will ask faith questions of their pastor and some fun questions of their teacher.

Luke 2:46

After three days they found him in the temple, sitting among the teachers, listening to them and asking them questions.

Getting Ready

Food: Your choice of lunch box drinks and single-serving snacks such as cheese and crackers, fruit or yogurt cups, and/or chips or cookies

Materials: Bible

For this activity plan to invite your pastor, lay minister, or director of Christian education. The kids will be invited to address Bible-based or faith questions to your guest, which may take about twenty minutes of his or her time.

Exploring the Story of Jesus at the Temple

Begin by welcoming your guest and saying a word about the guest's background. Have the kids introduce themselves.

Say: **When Jesus was a child, he was very interested in learning about his religion and exploring his faith in God. Today we're going to hear the story of twelve-year-old Jesus at the Temple. After the story you will have an opportunity to learn more about your Christian religion.**

Read Luke 2:41-52.

Say: **The story tells us that people at the Temple were amazed at Jesus' understanding. We want you to seek a good understanding of the Bible and your religion too. Just as Jesus asked questions. you may each ask a question or two of** (*your guest's name*)**.**

If the kids seem hesitant, you may initiate the question-and-answer session by asking a question kids often ask, such as; "Why did Jesus have to die?, "Where is heaven?, "Did Jesus have a brother and sister?" or "Why do we baptize people?"

After everyone who wants to has asked a question, thank your guest as you encourage the group to also say thanks.

Say: **Over the years I have learned from many teachers at church and at school. Of course I asked my teachers questions about my studies, but I also wanted to ask them fun questions about who they were as people too. For today's snack I've brought you lunch box foods in honor of schools and students and teachers. While you eat, I thought you might like to ask me questions about my childhood.**

Serve the snack and be prepared to tell the group about your favorite childhood color, flavor of ice cream, toy, television show, book, and so forth.

Pray: **All Knowing God, we thank you for students and teachers, questions and answers, church and school, and your son Jesus, who lives in our hearts and minds. Amen.**

If you could ask Jesus one question, what would it be?

FEEDING THE FIVE THOUSAND

LOAVES AND FISHES

Acting out the story, fixing fishy sandwiches, and crafting paper fish bring the miracle to life.

John 6:9

There is a boy here who has five barley loaves and two fish. But what are they among so many people?

Getting Ready

Food: Tuna salad; hoagie or sub rolls

Materials: Bible; knives; plates; copies of the skit; newspapers; scissors; markers; staplers (optional: sponge-painting materials or construction paper and glue

Bring the loaves (rolls) and fish (tuna salad) as separate ingredients, since kids will put the sandwiches together as part of the activity.

Kids will act out the story as a skit. You may want to invite another church group to see the skit after the kids have practiced it. Make photocopies of the skit for each child. Since you will need readers for the skit, if you have a group of all nonreaders, you may want to simply read or tell them the story.

Kids will create newspaper fish. Each paper fish will need three full sheets of newspaper, plus several sheets for stuffing.

Sharing the Story of the Loaves and Fishes

Begin by reading the story from John 6:1-14.
Say: Let's really bring this story to life by acting it out.
Select five readers, assembling the remaining kids as the crowd, and distributing copies of the skit to everyone. Give the actors a few minutes to study the script. Explain to the rest of the group that the skit will be performed twice: once as a dress rehearsal and once as the real show. (Let them know if they will be performing it for another group.) Place yourself with the kids who are in the crowd so that you can cue them and pantomime motions for them to imitate. Let the skit begin!

THE FEEDING OF THE FIVE THOUSAND

Narrator: Even though it is the sabbath, the Jewish day of rest, Jesus has been healing the sick. This angers some Jews, because he is not following the holy law. However, others believe that Jesus is obeying God's will. At this moment Jesus and his disciples have crossed the Sea of Galilee to sit on the mountainside.

Simon Peter: Look at all those people who have followed us! We'll never get any rest!

Andrew: Yes. They have seen Jesus perform many miracles today. They want to be near him.

Philip: There must be five thousand people coming up the hill!

Andrew: Where are we to buy bread for these people to eat?

Philip: Six months of wages would not buy enough bread for these people to have a little.

Andrew: There is a boy here who has five barley loaves and two fish. But what are they among so many people?

Jesus: Have the people sit down.

(The crowd sits down as the disciples walk over and speak.)

Simon Peter, Andrew, Philip: Please sit down, please sit down.

Narrator: Jesus takes the boy's bread and gives thanks for it. Then he blesses the fish and places the bread, then the fish, into baskets. He hands the food baskets to the disciples, and they go among the crowd.

(The disciples take imaginary baskets from Jesus and pretend to pass them among the crowd. The crowd pretends to take food, pass baskets, and eat.)

Jesus: Gather the fragments so that nothing may be lost.

(The disciples go back among the crowd to gather the baskets, then bring them to Jesus.)

Simon Peter: Look! There are twelve baskets of food!

Crowd: Another miracle! This is the prophet who is to come into the world!

The End

After the performances, invite the players to make sandwiches from your loaves and fish.

Pray: For miracles of fish and bread and five thousand people fed, for sandwiches we eat today, we give you thanks, O Lord, we pray. Amen.

As kids enjoy the snack, discuss how they might have felt if they had been eyewitnesses to the feeding of the five thousand.

Create large stuffed newspaper fish to decorate the room or the church, or for the kids to take home. Give each child three full sheets of newspaper, folded along the vertical crease. On the rectangular surface have kids use markers to draw a large oval to make the body of the fish. Next have them add a triangular tail fin that connects and overlaps one end of the oval. Fill the paper with as large a drawing as possible.

Have the kids staple around the edges, leaving a large opening for the mouth of the fish. With scissors have them cut around the stapled fish shape. Have them use their fingers to open the mouth of the fish and find the middle layer (three sheets of newspaper on the top and three on the bottom). Slide a hand in to open the fish's body, then stuff with wads of newspaper. Have the kids add eyes and scales with markers. For fancier fish consider sponge painting or glued construction paper eyes and scales.

What a way to feed a crowd!

ZACCHAEUS
BROCCOLI TREES

To understand that Jesus seeks to save us, act out the story of Zacchaeus by singing, climbing a yarn tree, and visiting his house for a snack of Broccoli Trees with Z's Cheese Dip.

Luke 19:4

So he ran ahead and climbed a sycamore tree to see him, because he was going to pass that way.

Getting Ready

Food: Bunches of fresh broccoli; Z's Cheese Dip

Recipe for Z's Cheese Dip: One 16-ounce container of cottage cheese; 3 tablespoons mayonnaise; 1½ teaspoons salt-free garlic and herb seasoning

Blend ingredients in food processor or blender. Refrigerate until time to serve. Yields two cups.

Materials: Bible; serving plate; small bowl; ball of yarn; food processor or blender

Wash the broccoli and cut it into spears. Arrange it on a serving plate with the bowl of dip.

With yarn create a simple tree outline. Make it as large as possible, so that later the kids may take turns climbing in the pretend tree.

Exploring the Story of Zacchaeus

Ask: Was there ever a time when you really wanted to see something such as a parade, a race, or a demonstration at a fair and you had to climb on something for a better view? (*Yes, I sat on the car hood; I climbed a fence.*)

Say: Usually we want to see because we are interested in what is going on or who is appearing. It was the same for a man named Zacchaeus. Listen to his story.

Read Luke 19:1-10.

Ask: Who did Zacchaeus want to see? (*Jesus*) **What did he climb in order to see Jesus?** (*a sycamore tree*) **Why did he climb the tree?** (*He was short and could not see over the crowd.*) **Even though there was a crowd gathered around Jesus, did Zacchaeus see him right away?** (*yes*) **Why were people angry when Jesus said he wanted to go to Zacchaeus' house?** (*He was a tax collector and probably had been taking their money unfairly.*) **Why do you think Jesus wanted to spend time with a sinner?** (*Jesus loves everyone, even sinners, and wants to bring them to God.*) **Did Zacchaeus change in response to Jesus?** (*Yes, he gave half of his money to the poor; he repaid those he had cheated.*)

Say: If we seek Jesus, then Jesus will find us. Our belief in him will help us become better people.

Sing the Zacchaeus song and act out the motions with gusto. (If no one knows the tune, say the lyrics along with the motions.)

Sing:

Zacchaeus was a wee little man, a wee little man was he,
(*Raise one palm over the other to indicate a small space.*)

He climbed up in a sycamore tree for the Lord he wanted to see,
(*Pretend to climb, then shade eyes to look for Jesus.*)

And as the Savior passed that way, He looked up in the tree,
(*Swing arms as if walking; shade eyes and look up.*)

And he said, Zacchaeus, you come down,
(*Motion with hand.*)

For I'm going to your house today, for I'm going to your house today.
(Clap in rhythm.)

Based on Luke 2:7.

After singing call the kids one at a time to "climb" the trunk of the yarn tree and stand in its branches.

Say: Come, *(child's name).* **You're invited to Zacchaeus' house.**

Send each child in turn to the snack table. Repeat until all are seated. Serve the snack and invite everyone to enjoy the Broccoli Trees and Z's Cheese Dip.

Conclude by asking the group to sit or stand in the yarn tree for prayer.

Pray: God of All People, we know that sometimes, like Zacchaeus, we do things that are wrong. We are glad to know that Jesus still cares for us and seeks to help us, no matter our sin. Amen.

Spelling challenge: close your eyes and spell Zacchaeus.

THE GOOD SAMARITAN
COMFORT FOODS

Creating get-well cards, forming a prayer huddle, and sharing a comfort food encourage us to think about what it means to be a good neighbor.

Luke 10:33

But a Samaritan while traveling came near him; and when he saw him, he was moved with pity.

Getting Ready

Food: Your choice of a comfort food such as chicken soup, macaroni and cheese, or mashed potatoes

Materials: Bible; blank notecards with matching envelopes; decorated adhesive bandage strips; crayons or markers; tape; bowls; spoons; serving bowls

Select a comfort food and purchase it ready-made or prepare it as directed.

Blank notecards with envelopes can be found in a craft or stationery store or in those departments of a general store. If you cannot locate blank notecards, purchase a box of envelopes with the tablet to match.

Ask your pastor or caregiving committee to help you make a list of the names of those who are sick at your church.

Exploring the Story of the Good Samaritan

Begin by asking the kids to talk about a time when they were sick or injured and someone helped make them feel better. Let the kids respond.

Say: When we are sick or injured, we need two kinds of care: care for the body and care for the spirit. First, we need kindhearted people to tend our bodies by bandaging a cut, setting a broken bone, cooling our fever, or feeding us spoonfuls of soup. Second, we need kindhearted people to lift our spirits by praying for us, visiting us, sending a get-well card, or bringing us a balloon or a joke book.

Continue: In the Bible there is a story about a man who helps an injured stranger. This man has become known as the Good Samaritan. Today there are hospitals, relief organizations, and even laws that use the word *Samaritan* in honor of the caregiver in this story.

Read Luke 10:25-37.

Say: In this story a lawyer talks to Jesus about how he can find eternal life in heaven. The two things necessary are to love God with all your heart, soul, and mind, and to love your neighbor. To help the lawyer understand what a neighbor is, Jesus tells the story of the Good Samaritan.

Ask: Did the Samaritan know who the injured man was? (*no*) Did he pass the stranger by? (*no*) How did the Samaritan help the man? (*He treated his wounds; he carried him to the inn; he paid the innkeeper to care for him.*) Which of the three men, the priest, the Levite, or the Samaritan, acted as a neighbor to the injured man? (*the Samaritan*) What does this story tell us that Jesus wants us to do? (*care for others even if they aren't really our next-door neighbors*)

Invite the group to be caring, good neighbors by coloring get-well cards for people in your church who need their spirits lifted. (You may want to go over the list of names to help kids understand who the recipients will be.) Give each child a notecard and an envelop to decorate as he or she wishes. After the cards are decorated, nonreaders may simply sign their names, while skilled readers can be encouraged to write a newsy or a poetic message.

As a finishing touch hand out a fancy bandage for kids to tape on each card. Then give everyone a bandage to keep handy in purses, wallets, or pockets. **Say: This will help you be a Good Samaritan along life's road.**

Gather your Samaritans into a huddle and ask them to repeat each line of the prayer after you.

Pray: God of heaven . . . As we walk . . . along life's roads . . . we'll help our neighbors . . . to carry their loads . . . when they're hurt . . . or when they're ill . . . we'll try our best . . . to do your will. Amen.

Serve the snack, explaining that this is a traditional food that people often like to eat when they want comfort. Encourage kids to tell the group what foods they like to each when they aren't feeling well in body and in spirit.

A cheery note can sometimes be the best medicine.

THE PRODIGAL SON
A WELCOME HOME PARTY

A rude guest disrupts the story of the Prodigal Son, but is forgiven, then welcomed to a party to honor God's forgiveness and our power to forgive.

Luke 15:20

So he set off and went to his father. But while he was still far off, his father saw him and was filled with compassion; he ran and put his arms around him and kissed him.

Getting Ready

Food: Favorite party foods such as pizza, chips and dip, and/or ice cream and cake

Materials: Bible; fancy paper plates; cups; napkins; tablecloth; rolls of crepe paper; tape

Invite someone such as a teenager, a parent, or a youth leader to play the role of the "prodigal." Ask your guest to plan on being disruptive as soon as you begin the activity by laughing, making little yet annoying noises or motions, trying to have side conversations with the kids, and so forth, until you ask him or her to leave. Later, the prodigal will return, ask to be forgiven, and then stay for the party.

Plan to have your group help you decorate and set out the foods for the party as part of the activity.

Exploring the Story of the Prodigal Son

Begin by welcoming the guest and encouraging him or her to take part in the activity. Start your introduction to the story, pausing occasionally to speak to your ill-mannered guest.

Say: In today's story Jesus is criticized by the Pharisees and scribes for eating a meal with sinners. Jesus tries to explain to them (*Pause to look with concern at your guest.*) that he cares very much for those who are wrongdoers. (*Glare at your guest.*) The lost have turned away from God's love and therefore do not treat others with love.

Say to the guest: I'm going to have to ask you to leave. It's hard for us to enjoy the story when you are disruptive. (*Guest leaves.*)

Continue: I'm sorry our guest couldn't stay, but it's not fair to you for our activity to be spoiled by bad behavior. Back to the story—Jesus hoped that the Pharisees and others would grasp his meaning through the story of the Prodigal Son.

Read Luke 15:11-24.

Ask: Does the returning son, also called the prodigal son, understand that he has behaved irresponsibly? (*yes*) Since his son has learned his lesson, is it right for the father to welcome him? (*Yes, our parents and God give us second chances.*) The father forgives his son, just as we forgive others. How should we show forgiveness to others? (*We can tell them; hug them; write a note; smile; or do something nice to show forgiveness.*)

Say: In the story the father gives a welcome home party, but there is a problem. Listen!

Read Luke 15:25-32.

Ask: Why is the brother who stayed home angry? (*As a good son, he believes he is not being treated fairly by his father.*) Do you think the angry brother realizes that the returning brother has changed for the better? (*not yet*) Does the father explain that he appreciates the son who stayed home? (*Yes, he would share every-thing with him.*) **Why does the father feel joy at the prodigal son's return?** (*He feels joy because his son was gone and has now returned. This son has a newly found respect and appreciation for his father.*)

Say: God, who is like the father in the story, will forgive us and welcome us home again.

Invite the group to celebrate the story of God's forgiveness by hosting a Prodigal Son Party. Have the kids join you in setting the table, hanging the crepe paper streamers, and preparing or bringing out party foods.

Invite the prodigal guest back into the room. After he or she has asked to be forgiven, enthusiastically invite the prodigal to the party.

Praise God for the grace of forgiveness!

Pray: Forgiving God, help us remember to ask for forgiveness when we are wrong and to lovingly extend our forgiveness to others. We celebrate in Jesus' name. Amen.

Enjoy your snack. Invite your prodigal guest to be first in line.

PENTECOST
A BIRTHDAY CAKE FOR THE CHURCH

Celebrate the birthday of the church by decorating a cake, playing a party game, singing a birthday song, and hearing the story of Pentecost.

Acts 2:42

They devoted themselves to the apostles' teaching and fellowship, to the breaking of bread and the prayers.

Getting Ready

Food: A frosted cake; one or two small tubes of colored frosting; edible decorations such as gum drops, sprinkles, and/or mini-morsels

Materials: Bible; birthday candles; cake knife; plates; forks; lighter or matches

For this celebration the kids will decorate the cake by writing "Happy Birthday" on it with frosting and embellishing it with edible decorations.

Exploring the Story of Pentecost

Begin with the Birthday Stand Up Game. To play, individuals stand up and sit down again quickly when you say something that is true about their own birthdays. First, ask kids to stand up when you call out their birthday month. Next, have them stand up if they are the first born in the family, then the second, third, fourth, fifth. Lastly, have them stand on the date they were born (first, second, third . . .)

Say: **Today we're celebrating a birthday, but it's not the birthday of a person; it's the birthday of the Christian church. This day is called "Pentecost." After the Holy Spirit came upon the apostles in a mighty wind, many recognized that God was with them and had given them special wisdom and power. Here is the story.**

Read Acts 2:41-47.

Ask: **How many people were baptized on Pentecost?** (*three thousand*) **What did the first Christians do together?** (*listened to the apostles' teachings, broke bread, and prayed*) **The word** *fellowship* **is not explained in the story. Does anyone know what it means?** (*being companions; sharing a common interest*) **What about "breaking bread?"** (*This means breaking into a loaf of bread, but it also means eating together.*)

Say: **Just like the first Christians, we are listening to teachings, sharing fellowship, breaking bread, and praying with one another. And that's a wonderful way to celebrate the birthday of the church. However, what's a birthday without a cake? I've brought a cake for you to decorate!**

Bring out the cake and make sure to distribute the edible decorations so that each child has some.

When the cake has received its finishing touches, admire the beautiful results and then ask the kids to bow their heads for prayer.

Pray: **Holy God, thank you for birthdays and candles and cake and parties. Most of all, thank you for our birthdays and for Pentecost, the birthday of the Christian church. Amen.**

Next, light the candles on the cake, then ask the group to create a mighty wind to blow them out. Have the children sing "Happy Birthday" to the church.

Serve the cake and enjoy fellowship.

Another ring around the tree, another orbit of the sun, another candle on a cake, another year has just begun.

ADVENT

STIR-UP SUNDAY

Celebrate the start of Advent with the centuries-old tradition of making Stir-up Sunday Cakes.

Isaiah 40:5

Then the glory of the LORD shall be revealed, and all people shall see it together, for the mouth of the LORD has spoken.

Getting Ready

Foods: Stir-up Sunday Cakes

Materials: Bible; muffin pans; paper baking cups; mixing bowl; large spoon; small ladle

Stir-up Sunday is the Sunday before the first Sunday of Advent, although this activity will work well anytime during Advent.

To make Stir-up Sunday Cakes, prepare a spice or carrot cake batter from scratch or from a mix. Kids will stir in about two cups of candied fruit. A standard recipe or cake mix should yield about 24 cupcakes.

While the Stir-up Sunday Cakes are baking and cooling (around fifteen to twenty minutes), you may want to have the kids make Advent calendars or other decorations, sing Christmas carols, or listen to Christmas stories.

Celebrating Advent

Say: Soon it will be the season of the church year that we call "Advent." The word *Advent* means "coming." We are getting ready for the coming of Jesus at Christmas.

Explain that even in Old Testament times, the Hebrew people were waiting for the coming of Jesus. Read Isaiah 40:5.

Say: We don't know the exact day of Jesus' birth, but around the fifth century the date of December 25 was set. As the custom of celebrating Christmas grew, Christians decided that they needed a time of spiritual preparation to get ready for the celebration. That's when the season of Advent began.

Invite kids to take turns telling traditions they enjoy during Advent, both at church and at home.

Say: Years ago the Sunday before the first Sunday of Advent was called "Stir-up Sunday." This name was inspired by the opening words of a prayer said on that day. The words are: "Stir up we beseech thee, O Lord, the wills of thy faithful people." Stir-up Sunday became the day that folks began to stir up Christmas treats, especially a special Christmas cake made with candied fruit. All members of the household would take a turn stirring the batter. As each person stirred, he or she made a wish. After the cake was finished, it was packed away until Christmas.

Tell the kids that they are now going to make Stir-up Sunday Cakes. Bring out the cake batter. Let them each take a small handful of the candied fruit, one at a time, and stir it into the batter. As they stir, encourage them to make a wish. Ladle the batter into the paper baking cups set into the muffin pans.

While the Stir-up Sunday Cakes bake, lead the kids in another activity or encourage them to discuss their holiday plans.

Pray: Dear God, as we stir up treats this Advent season, we pray that you will stir up our hearts and make them ready for the coming of your son, Jesus, at Christmas. Amen.

As the kids taste and comment on the cakes, remind them that they are lucky. Years ago children would have had to wait until Christmas to try the Stir-up Sunday Cake that they helped make.

What is your wish for this Advent season?

CHRISTMAS CAROLING
WHITE HOT CHOCOLATE

After participating in an old Christmas tradition, carolers will be rewarded with a brand new treat.

Luke 2:13-14

And suddenly there was with the angel a multitude of the heavenly host, praising God and saying, "Glory to God in the highest heaven, and on earth peace among those whom he favors!"

Getting Ready

Food: White Christmas Hot Chocolate; small candy canes; Christmas cookies or other treats

Materials: Pot; ladle; Bible; serving plates; plates; napkins; song sheets, hymnals, or songbooks; mugs or hot cups (optional: holiday tablecloth and table decorations)

These holiday refreshments are a warm way to welcome returning carolers. If the caroling is to be done out of the church, arrange for helpers and transportation, if needed. If this isn't practical, you may want to simply send kids caroling around the church during the Sunday school hour.

Caroling works best with an enthusiastic song leader and copies of the lyrics for carolers. If you will be caroling at night, don't forget flashlights so readers can see the words.

You may choose to make the White Christmas Hot Chocolate at home and then warm it at church, or mix it at church.

For a small group: ¾ cup water; 8 ounces white chocolate morsels; ¼ cup sugar; ¼ teaspoon salt; 4½ cups milk; 1 teaspoon vanilla. Yields 8 5-ounce cups.

For a crowd: 2¼ cups water; 24 ounces white chocolate morsels; ¾ cups sugar; ¾ teaspoons salt; 14 cups milk; 3 teaspoons vanilla. Yields 25 5-ounce cups.

Heat water to boiling. Reduce heat. Mix in sugar, salt, and chocolate pieces. Stir constantly until chocolate is melted. Add milk. Continue to stir gently to prevent scorching. Remove from heat and add vanilla. Reheat as needed. Add candy canes as festive stirrers.

To go along with the hot chocolate, prepare a plate or plates of holiday treats. Arrange and decorate the serving table.

Celebrating Christmas

Gather the kids together. Begin by welcoming them.

Ask: On the first Christmas, when Jesus was born, who do you think sang the first Christmas carol? (*the angels who sang to the shepherds*)

Read Luke 2:13-14.

Next give a bit of background information on the history of Christmas carols.

Say: In a few minutes you will be taking part in an old tradition, the tradition of Christmas caroling. When you return, you are going to be served a brand new treat! (*The treat is to be kept a surprise.*) **The word** *carol* **comes from the Greek word** *choraulein*, **which means "a dance accompanied by flute music." This traditional dance was taken on by early Christians, although over time they dropped the dancing and the flute music and just sang songs that they called "carols." At first carols were sung not only at Christmas but at Easter and other seasons of the church year, but today we just sing carols at Christmas.**

Hand out the song sheets. (Nonreaders may want to carry them, even if they can't really read them.) Have the kids warm up by leading them in a carol. Remind them again that when they return, they will be rewarded with a brand new treat.

Pray: Dear God, help us to sing our very best, so that we can spread Christmas joy to all who hear our carols. Amen.

When the caroling is finished, have the group gather around the table. Hold up a cup of the hot chocolate with a candy cane stirrer.

Say: This brand new treat is White Christmas Hot Chocolate. Usually hot chocolate is made with chocolate that is brown, but this hot chocolate is white to remind us of snow!

Serve the hot chocolate. As you hand carolers their cups, remind them that the chocolate is hot. Serve the Christmas treats too, and encourage carolers to talk about the happy reception their singing received.

Hark, how did your angels sing?

THE NEW YEAR
BE GLAD AND REJOICE

Celebrate God's gift of life with a countdown, noisemakers, popcorn confetti, and a taste of traditional New Year foods.

Psalm 32:11

Be glad in the LORD and rejoice, O righteous, and shout for joy, all you upright in heart.

Getting Ready

Food: Traditional New Year's foods; popcorn (popped for the snack and unpopped kernels for craft); beverage

Materials: Bible; serving bowls; cups; plates; spoons; white paper plates; stapler; crayons; (optional: crepe paper streamers)

Even if New Year's Eve has already come or hasn't quite arrived, kids will enjoy this celebration, which doesn't need to take place at midnight, but can be done anytime of the day or night!

Plan on serving some traditional New Year foods such as black-eyed peas, herring, and/or cooked greens such as collard or spinach. Since kids aren't usually overly fond of those foods, you will probably just need small portions. Popcorn, which will also be tossed as confetti and left for the birds, will make a more substantial snack.

You will need at least two serving bowls filled with popcorn. Arrange the New Year's foods in bowls too.

Kids will construct New Year 's Tambourines for the celebration. Make a sample to show them by using crayons to decorate two paper plates. Put a handful of popcorn kernels on the reverse side of one, then staple the plates together along the edges. You may want to staple lengths of crepe paper (about eight inches) to the edges of the tambourine to make streamers.

Celebrating the New Year

Say: **We are going to pretend that this is New Year's Eve and hold a New Year's celebration.** (*You may want to make a comment about when the real new year did begin or will begin.*)
Read Psalm 32:11.
Say: **Many Christians feel that when we pray and offer our thanks to God, we need to pray calmly and quietly. This verse**

tells us that it's OK to praise God with loud shouts of joy. When we celebrate the coming of the new year, we are praising God with loud shouts of joy as we anticipate a brand new year.

Have kids create their New Year Tambourines. When they are finished, announce that the time for the New Year celebration has come. Explain that you will be counting down to the new year twice. Once outdoors and once indoors.

Have kids leave their tambourines inside. Guide them outdoors, bringing along one of the bowls of popcorn. Explain that the popcorn is Popcorn Confetti. After they toss the confetti, it will be left on the ground as a snack for the birds. Ask each child to take a handful to hold onto until after the countdown.

Say: I will count down to midnight, just like we do on the real New Year's Eve. Then we'll shout "Happy New Year' and toss our confetti as high in the air as we possibly can. Ready? Ten, nine, eight, seven, six, five, four, three, two, one, Happy New Year!

If there is Popcorn Confetti left in the bowl, encourage kids to toss that too, then lead them back indoors.

Point out the traditional New Year's foods, explaining that in many places, it is considered good luck for these to be the first foods eaten in the new year. Tell the kids that after the next pretend midnight, you will serve the foods. Have them pick up their New Year's Tambourines and lead them through another countdown to midnight.

Before you serve the New Year's foods, ask the kids to bow their heads.

Pray: Dear God, we remember the old years, and we celebrate the new year and we thank you the joy of life. Amen.

Serve the traditional foods, encouraging kids to try them, even if they only take tiny tastes. Then serve the popcorn and beverage.

Say a thank-you prayer to God for a new year.

ST. VALENTINE'S DAY
HEART-SHAPED PIZZAS

Craft Christian valentines to send to those in your congregation who need a bit of loving cheer; then enjoy a heart-shaped snack.

1 Corinthians 13:4-5

Love is patient; love is kind; love is not envious or boastful or arrogant or rude. It does not insist on its own way; it is not irritable or resentful.

Getting Ready

Foods: Valentine Pizzas

Materials: Bible; spoon; envelopes; baking sheets; knife; bowls; plates; colored paper; white paper; paper doilies; scissors; glue; markers or crayons (optional: fabric and/or craft trimmings)

You can prepare the Valentine Pizzas before kids arrive, or have them help you as part of the activity. Toppings are optional, although they add to the fun and flavor. Set any toppings into bowls.

Recipe for Valentine Pizzas: English muffins; spaghetti or pizza sauce; shredded mozzarella cheese; optional toppings for pizza such as mushrooms, pepperoni, cooked sausage; and/or black olives

Preheat oven to 375 degrees. With a knife split muffins and cut a one-inch triangular wedge from each to create a heart shape. Toast for two or three minutes until they begin to crisp. Remove from oven and spoon one or two tablespoons of sauce on each. Sprinkle with about two tablespoons of mozzarella cheese. Return to oven until the cheese has melted. After the pizzas are baked, toppings can be added to the pizzas by each individual .

Kids will create valentines to mail or to be delivered to those in your congregation who need a bit of cheer. Consider the older members, the sick, the grieving, and any newcomers to the congregation. Consult with your pastor or caregiving committee.

Before the kids arrive, set out the supplies for making the paper valentines. Write some of the phrases from the Bible reading on the board or on a large piece of paper for the readers to copy onto their valentines.

Celebrating Valentine's Day

Begin by reading 1 Corinthians 13:4-7.

Then say: This is one of the most famous passages in the Bible. The passage talks about the qualities of love.

Read the passage again, pausing to ask kids to give examples of the qualities listed. For example, **say: Tell me a time when you showed love by being patient.** (*When my little brother kept begging me to teach him how to tie his shoes.*)

Finish discussing the passage.

Ask: Can anyone tell me what holiday is a special celebration of love? (*Valentine's Day*)

Next give a brief history of the holiday.

Say: Valentine's Day goes back to ancient times, when people held a festival called "Lupercalia' on February 14. Couples often paired up on this day. In the third century the day was renamed in honor of an Italian priest, Valentine. Later made a saint, Valentine was known for his kind words and loving deeds. By the 1800's the invention of the printing press made it possible for companies to produce lots of valentine cards. But folks still like to make their own, which is what we are going to do today.

Explain that the valentines the kids make will be mailed to those in your congregation especially in need of loving greetings. (You may want to name some of those people.) Show kids the craft supplies, inviting them to create lovely valentines. If you have readers, point out the phrases from the Bible, suggesting they add them to their cards.

While kids are working, either bake the pizzas or set out the ingredients so that the kids can help.

When the valentine cards are finished, announce that now it's time for kids to enjoy valentines that can be eaten. Either serve them the baked valentine pizzas or set them to work creating their own. Invite kids to add toppings, if you have them, to the baked pizzas.

Before kids devour the snack, ask them to hold their hands over their heads, tipping their fingers downward to form the top of a heart.

Pray: Give us loving hearts today, bless these valentines on their way, and thanks for pizza, Lord, we pray. Amen.

Mail the valentines or ask your pastor or caregiving group to deliver them during visitations.

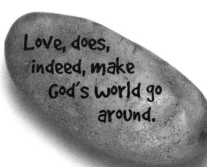

Love, does, indeed, make God's world go around.

LENT
PANCAKE TUESDAY

Mark the beginning of Lent with a Pancake Race, followed by a pile of pancakes.

Mark 1:13

He was in the wilderness forty days, tempted by Satan; and he was with the wild beasts; and the angels waited on him.

Getting Ready

Foods : Pancakes; butter; syrup; juice

Materials: Several frying pans; a bell; plates; cups; knives; forks; (optional: crepe paper streamers or construction paper)

Plan on cooking pancakes at church or making them ahead of time and reheating them at church. You may want to purchase frozen pancakes. Keep the pancakes warm during the race so that they are ready when the racing is finished. Consider recruiting a helper to make this easier.

In the Pancake Race kids will race along a course you determine (outdoors works best). Mark the race route, if necessary, with crepe paper streamers or paper signs. If possible, the race should end at the door of the church. At the finish racers will be greeted by the bellringer, who will begin ringing a bell as soon as he or she sees the racers approaching. If you have an actual church bell that kids might be permitted to ring, this is a fine time to use it. Otherwise a hand bell will do. The size of your group and the number of frying pans you can locate will determine how many kids will race at one time.

Just before the activity begins, place a pancake in each frying pan.

Celebrating Lent

Gather the kids together. Hold up one of the frying pans.

Ask: What's this? (*a frying pan with a pancake in it*) **How many of you have had pancakes in the last two weeks?**

Say: Pancakes have always been a popular food. But years ago people did not eat pancakes during Lent.

Ask: Can anyone tell me what Lent is? (*the forty-day time period before Easter*)

Say: Lent is the season of the church year that comes before Easter. The word *Lent* is derived from an Old English word *lengten*, which means "spring." The forty-day time period comes from the forty days that Jesus spent in the wilderness before he began his ministry.

Read Mark 1:13.

Say: Years ago, during Lent, as a reminder that Jesus suffered before he died on the cross, people gave up sweets and fats and eggs during Lent. On the Tuesday before Lent begins on Ash Wednesday, they would use up all of those ingredients. One way to do this was to make pancakes.

Continue: Since Lent was such a solemn time, the day before Lent began, sometimes called "Fat Tuesday' or "Mardi Gras," became a day of fun and games. One of those games was the Pancake Race. At the sound of the church bell, women rushed from their houses with a freshly made pancake in their frying pan. When the first woman reached the church, the bellringer ate her pancake and gave her a kiss.

Announce that kids will now take part in a genuine Pancake Race. Boys, as well as girls, will run in your race. Decide on who will race first, hand them frying pans, and choose a bellringer. Explain that the bellringer will stand at the finish and ring the bell when the racers come into sight and keep ringing it until the first racer arrives. The bellringer is to take a bite of the racer's pancake, then give the winner a kiss! (For each race, chose a different bellringer.)

Send the bellringer to the finishing place. Start the race by saying: "Racers on your mark, get set, go." The rest of the group may stand along the race route, with a clear view of the finishing place.

When everyone has had a turn to participate in the race, call the kids together.

Say: I hope that all of this racing has made you hungry for pancakes!

Pray: Dear God, we're glad for traditions such as Pancake Races, and we're glad for piles of pancakes. This year during Lent help us to remember that Jesus gave his life for us. Amen.

Let the kids enjoy their pancakes.

On your mark, get set, relax. No more Pancake Races until next year!

EASTER
EMPTY TOMB ROLLS

Rolls with a surprise, and a surprise to take home, draw us into the wonder of the empty tomb.

Luke 24:2-3
They found the stone rolled away from the tomb, but when they went in, they did not find the body.

Getting Ready

Foods: Empty Tomb Rolls

Materials: Bible; baking sheets; modeling dough; reclosable food storage bags (optional: book below)

When the Empty Tomb Rolls are baked, the marshmallow melts and there is a space inside. This is the empty tomb! Since some of the marshmallow may melt onto the baking sheet, it's best to remove rolls promptly to prevent them from sticking.

Recipe for Empty Tomb Rolls: Canned biscuit dough; large marshmallows; cinnamon sugar; melted butter.

Shape each biscuit around a marshmallow, pinching the edges together and sealing them as tightly as possible. Dip biscuit in butter, then roll it in cinnamon sugar. Place the biscuit, seam side down, on a greased baking sheet. Bake at 350 until lightly browned.

You may choose to bake the rolls at home or at church. Although they are best served warm, you can serve them unheated if need be.

Each child will receive a reclosable bag with modeling dough inside. During the activity they will create empty tombs using the modeling dough. Consider making dough using the directions below, or simply purchase modeling dough.

To make modeling dough: Mix one cup flour with 1/2 cup salt. Add food coloring to a cup of water and two tablespoons cooking oil. Stir into dry ingredients and heat over medium heat for several minutes. Let cool and then knead until smooth.

Put portions of the modeling dough into the food storage bags and seal the bags. Kids will be invited to take the modeling dough home with them at the end of the activity.

You may want to read *One Morning in Joseph's Garden: An Easter Story* by Barbara Younger and Lisa Flinn (Abingdon Press, 1998) to the kids during this activity.

Celebrating Easter

As soon as the kids are settled, serve them the rolls.

Ask: What's different about these rolls? (*They are hollow inside.*)

Say: These are called Empty Tomb Rolls.

Ask: Do you know whose empty tomb they are named for? (*the tomb where Jesus was buried*)

Say: In Bible days people were often buried in tombs. Jesus was buried in a tomb in the garden of a wealthy man named Joseph.

Read the story of the Resurrection of Jesus (Luke 24:1-12).

Ask: What did the women first notice when they arrived at the tomb? (*The stone was rolled away.*) **What was the reaction of the women when they realized the tomb was empty?** (*They were perplexed, which means they did not understand.*) **Who helped them understand that Jesus had really risen from the dead?** (*men in dazzling clothes*) **Then what did the women do?** (*They told the disciples and others.*)

Say: The women and the disciples were happy and amazed that the tomb was empty and that Jesus had risen from the dead. This is the great news of the Resurrection that we celebrate at Easter.

Have kids bow their heads for a prayer of celebration.

Pray: God of the Resurrection, we celebrate the great news of the empty tomb. Alleluia! Jesus has risen! Amen.

Give kids the bags of modeling dough. Explain that this is a surprise for them to take home, but first they are to use the dough to create the tomb of Jesus and the stone that was rolled away from the entrance.

When the creations are finished, take a few minutes to admire them before inviting kids to pack the dough away.

Alleluia! The tomb is empty! He is risen indeed!

MIDSUMMER
A WATERMELON FEST

Gathering together for outdoor games and watermelon reminds us of the joy of the seasons.

Genesis 8:22

As long as the earth endures, seedtime and harvest, cold and heat, summer and winter, day and night, shall not cease.

Getting Ready

Food: Watermelon

Materials: Sharp knife; paper plates; forks; large serving spoons; Bible; beach balls or other balls

Plan this activity for the outdoors, although games may be moved indoors in case of rain or extreme heat. This is a good time to invite other groups of kids, parents, and/or grandparents. Although years ago Midsummer was observed in late June, you can celebrate summer anytime during the season.

You may want to set up for volleyball or croquet, provide a splashing center with water toys, and/or supply bubbles and bubble wands.

These traditional games have been adapted to fit the theme of the celebration:

Duck, Duck, Summer: A seasonal variation of Duck, Duck, Goose. The person who is "It' taps others on the head saying, "Fall, Winter, Spring, Summer." The rules for Duck, Duck, Goose apply, although instead of being sent to the "Stew Pot," the person who is caught is tossed into the "Swimming Pool" (the center of the circle).

Summer on a Spoon: A beach ball or other ball is carried on a spoon in a relay race during this variation of Potato on a Spoon. With younger kids you may want to use large serving spoons. Older kids will enjoy the challenge of balancing the ball on a small spoon.

Summer, May I?: In this variation of Mother, May I, the person playing Summer makes up directions relating to summer such as "Jump three big waves in the ocean," "Take six baby hops across the park," or "Take two diving leaps into the pool."

Season Tag: In this variation of Freeze Tag, players are safe from being frozen if they shout out the name of a season before they are tagged.

Celebrating Midsummer

Gather the kids together. Tell them you are going to hold a clapping and shouting contest to see which is their favorite season. Appoint someone to be the judge. Say the name of each season and let kids clap and shout for their favorites. Then ask the judge which season was the winner. (If you live in an area where the seasons don't change drastically, you may want to point out your seasonal changes.)

Say: Even though most of us have a favorite season, God had a reason for creating each season. Seasons are part of God's plan for the earth.

Read Genesis 8:22.

Continue: Today we've gathered to celebrate Midsummer. Years ago this holiday was celebrated in late June, in honor of the longest day of the year. But anytime is a good time to celebrate summer!

Ask the kids to gather in a circle and join hands. Have them walk slowly in one direction.

Pray: Dear God, just as the earth goes round and round, the seasons of the year do too. We're glad for the earth, we're glad for seasons, and we're especially glad for you. Amen.

Just how far can you spit a watermelon seed?

Lead kids in games and any other activities you have planned. You may want to take a break and serve the watermelon, or serve it when the games are over.

WORLD COMMUNION SUNDAY
BREAD FROM MANY LANDS

Tasting the daily bread of many lands makes us mindful of Christians throughout the world who are united in faith.

1 Corinthians 10:17

Because there is one bread, we who are many are one body, for we all partake of the one bread.

Getting Ready

Food: A variety of breads; grape juice (optional: spreads)

Materials: Bible; baskets or bowls; plates; cups; (optional: decorations and/or international music and player)

World Communion Sunday, the first Sunday in October, is celebrated by churches throughout the world. If your church observes World Communion Sunday, you may want to tie in this activity, or use the activity anytime during the year as a discussion of Holy Communion and Christian unity.

Plan on serving at least three or four varieties of international breads. Pita bread, rye bread, tortillas, French bread, and Italian bread can be found in most food stores. Depending on where you live, your stores may stock other international breads. Perhaps there are members of your congregation who would be happy to bake breads that are part of their cultural backgrounds.

Although not necessary, kids will enjoy having spreads such as butter, cream cheese, jam, and humus. to put on the breads.

Decorations will add to the international flavor. Consider tablecloths, dolls, flags, musical instruments, or other artifacts from another land. Musical recordings such as a Jamaican or Irish band will also enhance the international atmosphere.

Before the activity begins, slice breads and place them in baskets or bowls. Set out the spreads, if you have them, and the grape juice. Arrange any decorations.

Celebrating World Communion Sunday

If you have music, play it as the kids arrive.

Say: Look at the variety of breads we have here today.

Ask kids to tell you what kinds of bread there are, if they can. Say the names of those they do not know.

Continue: Every year churches celebrate World Communion Sunday on the first Sunday in October. (*Explain how World Communion Sunday is observed at your church, if you celebrate it.*) **On this Sunday Christians all over the world partake of Holy Communion. This reminds us that even though we come from different cultures, speak different languages, eat different foods, and have different customs, we are all one in the body of Christ.**

Read 1 Corinthians 10:17.

Have kids bow their heads.

Pray: God of All Nations, we thank you for our Christian sisters and brothers throughout the world. As we sample these breads today, help us to remember that we are all one in the body of Christ. Amen.

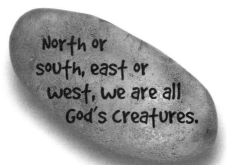

North or south, east or west, we are all God's creatures.

Serve the breads, any spreads that you have brought, and grape juice. Play music again if you have it, and encourage kids to examine and ask questions about any international artifacts.

ALL SOULS' DAY
A CLASS COOKBOOK

Creating a class cookbook helps us honor and remember our loved ones.

Romans 8:38-39

For I am convinced that neither death, nor life, nor angels, nor rulers, nor things present, nor things to come, nor powers, nor height, nor depth, nor anything else in all creation, will be able to separate us from the love of God in Christ Jesus our Lord.

Getting Ready

Foods: A snack prepared from a family recipe

Materials: White paper; Bible; crayons; folders

Traditionally, All Saints' Day and the day after, All Souls' Day (November 2), are days to remember departed loved ones. This activity is designed to help kids understand that even though we lose people we love through death, they still live within us in many ways.

To kick off the cookbook project, plan on preparing a recipe passed down from one of your departed loved ones, such as your grandmother's coffee cake or your great-aunt's noodles.

Kids will then be asked to bring in a recipe to contribute to a class cookbook. The recipes don't necessarily have to be those of a departed loved one. Any favorite family recipe will be fine. They will make simple Recipe Reminders using crayons and white paper, but it would be wise to say a word to parents too.

Recipes may be handwritten or typed on 8½-by-11-inch paper. After the recipes are turned in to you at church, the pages will be photocopied. One simple way to bind the cookbook is to slip the pages into a folder that has a clear cover and plastic sleeves.

Each child will want a cookbook to take home but consider making copies for other groups in your church or even the entire church.

Celebrating All Saints' Day

Say: Today I have a snack that is very dear to me because the recipe comes from someone who was very dear to me. (*Give a bit of information about whose recipe it is and why that person is still dear to you, even though he or she is no longer living. Try to include some of the qualities that made that person unique.*)

Let the kids enjoy the snack.

Ask: Have any of you had a loved one die? (*Encourage those who are comfortable to share their memories of that person.*)

Say: The Bible tells us that nothing, not even death, can ever separate us from the love of God through Jesus.

Read Romans 8:38-39.

Continue: Just as death will not separate us from God, when someone we love dies, that person is still with us in many ways. We have memories of the person and we have traditions, such as favorite recipes, that have been passed along to us. All Soul's Day is a day set aside on the Christian calendar each year to honor and remember those loved ones who have died. Another way to remember those who have died is in our prayers.

Tell the kids that you will now say a prayer, leaving a period of silence for them to remember their own loved ones who have died.

Pray: Dear God, we are glad that death will never separate us from you. We are also glad that you have given us memories and traditions to help us remember loved ones who have died. Hear us as we silently say their names to you now (*pause*) **We pray this prayer in the name of Jesus. Amen.**

Next, explain the cookbook project. Tell kids that the recipes don't have to be from someone who has died, although they certainly may be. However, they do need to be the recipe of someone they love. Explain that they, or a family member, are to write or type the recipe on 8½-by-11-inch plain white paper. (Remind them that this is standard printer size.) Encourage them to decorate their recipe pages too. Give a date when you want the recipes returned and explain who will receive the finished cookbook. You may want to work together to come up with a creative title for the cookbook.

Hand kids a sheet of white paper, asking them to color and/or write a Recipe Reminder for themselves.

After the kids bring in their recipes, photocopy and collate them and bind the cookbook together. Encourage kids to take the cookbooks home and to try preparing one another's recipes, with the help of their parents.

Bon appetit to you and yours!

GIVING THANKS
PUMPKIN PIE CUPS

Mix up a batch of our many blessings in the Thanksgiving Prayer Pot and then make a batch of tasty Pumpkin Pie Cups.

Psalm 92:1

It is good to give thanks to the LORD, to sing praises to your name, O Most High.

Getting Ready

Food: Pumpkin Pie Cups

Materials: Nine-ounce clear plastic cups; a large spoon; spoons; mixing bowls; markers or crayons; Bible; slips of colored paper; pot

For the prayer activity kids will write down their blessings on slips of paper and place them into the Thanksgiving Prayer Pot. Readers will be able to record blessings faster than nonreaders. Count on about three or four slips of paper for nonreaders and six to ten for readers. Paper in a variety of colors will make the pot look more festive.

Kids will prepare the snack as part of the activity.

Recipe for Pumpkin Pie Cups: one 15-ounce can pumpkin; one cup sugar; two 8-ounce containers whipped topping; one teaspoon cinnamon; ½ teaspoon nutmeg; graham cracker crumbs

Place the graham cracker crumbs into a mixing bowl and set them aside. Have kids help combine pumpkin and sugar in another mixing bowl, then stir in one container of the whipped topping and the spices. Next, give each child a cup and spoon. Have kids put a spoonful or two of crumbs into their cups. Then you will use the large spoon to put a heaping spoonful of the pumpkin mixture into each cup. Kids will add another layer of crumbs, and you will top with the plain whipped topping.

Celebrating Thanksgiving

Begin by asking kids to tell their favorite part of Thanksgiving dinner.

Say: Thanksgiving is an occasion when we enjoy wonderful foods. But most of all, Thanksgiving is a time to thank God for the many blessings in our lives. In celebration we are going to stir our blessings into the Thanksgiving Prayer Pot.

Ask kids to write down one blessing per slip of paper. Nonreaders will need assistance. The kids are then to put the slips of paper into the pot, saying as they do, "Thank you, God, for all of my blessings." Once the blessings are all in the pot, stir the pot with the spoon and tip it to the side for all to see.

Tell kids to close their eyes while you read Psalm 92:1-4.

Conclude: Thank you God, for this pot full of blessings.

Next, announce that in celebration of delicious Thanksgiving foods, kids will be making Pumpkin Pie Cups. Following the recipe, have kids put the Pumpkin Pie Cups together. Before they enjoy the snack, lead them in singing "Praise God, from Whom All Blessings Flow."

Praise God, from Whom All Blessings Flow

Praise God, from whom all blessings flow;
praise him, all creatures here below;
praise him above, ye heavenly host;
Father, Son, and Holy Ghost. Amen.

Words by Thomas Ken, 1674.

o give thanks to the Lord, for God is good.

SHARING GOD'S BOUNTY

GROUP SOUP
STRIVING SIDE BY SIDE

Work together to cook up a pot of the best vegetable soup ever!

Philippians 1:27

Only, live your life in a manner worthy of the gospel of Christ, so that, whether I come and see you or am absent and hear about you, I will know that you are standing firm in one spirit, striving side by side with one mind for the faith of the gospel.

Getting Ready

Food: Group Soup; crackers

Materials: Large soup pot; ladle; can openers; bowls or cups; spoons; Bible

In this activity kids will prepare Group Soup for an occasion at your church such as a workday, church luncheon, or dinner meeting. While the soup may taste best if allowed to mellow a bit, it may also be served soon after it is prepared. Decide to whom you will offer your delicious soup and when it will be served.

Send home notices or make phone calls asking kids to each bring a frozen or canned vegetable to contribute to the soup. You may want to have some additional vegetables on hand, in the event that kids forget to bring vegetables and to assure variety and quantity.

At home, prepare the base for the soup. (You may choose to leave out the meat.)

65

Soup Base: 3 quarts water; 3 cans (11¾ ounces) beef stock; 3 pounds hamburger, browned; garlic and/or chopped onion; black pepper; salt

Put ingredients into a large soup pot and simmer for fifteen minutes. Cool and refrigerate until it's time to make the soup.

Bring along herbs such as parsley, sage, basil, and thyme for kids to add to taste as the soup cooks, along with salt and pepper. You also may want to have some bouillon or soup starter on hand.

It's a good idea to recruit a teenage or adult helper to monitor the soup on the stove.

While the soup simmers, plan on leading the kids in another activity in which they can work side by side for the church. Consider having them make bulletin covers or get-well cards, or perhaps straighten and clean an area of the church.

Sharing Group Soup

After the kids arrive, invite them to follow you to the kitchen. Older ones can open their cans or packages of frozen vegetables; you may need to assist younger ones. Have kids carefully put their undrained vegetables into the soup, then use the ladle to stir them in. If the soup seems too thick, add more water. Finally, let kids add spices.

Your helper can begin to cook the soup while you gather the kids together for the discussion and an additional activity.

Say: We've just worked together to make what I think will be a very delicious soup. We're going to call it Group Soup, since our group made it.

Explain when the soup will be served and who will get the chance to enjoy it.

Then say: As Christians we are called to work together. Listen to what Paul wrote about working together in one of his letters to an early Christian church.

Read Philippians 1:27.

Ask: What are some of the ways that we work together side by side as Christians here at our church? (*sing in the youth choir; help rake the church lawn; decorate for Christmas*)

Next, ask the kids to stand in a line, side by side, and have them link elbows.

Pray: Dear God, here we are striving side by side for the faith of the gospel. Help us to strive with one mind and spirit to do the work of your church. Amen.

Lead kids in the additional activity you have decided upon.

After this is done, take them back into the kitchen. Ladle a small amount of soup for each child, making certain kids understand that the soup is hot and can burn. Serve crackers along with the soup. As they taste, invite opinions on the soup. Perhaps it needs more spices? Some bouillon or soup starter to give it a stronger flavor? Make any adjustments necessary.

Soup's on! Get it while it's hot!

If kids are not present when the Group Soup is served, make sure they hear some of the wonderful compliments it will no doubt receive!

A CRAYON DRIVE
GOD'S WORLD of COLOR

Acclaim God's world of color with a rainbow snack, crayon projects, and a drive to collect new boxes of crayons for a local shelter.

Genesis 9:13

I have set my bow in the clouds, and it shall be a sign of the covenant between me and the earth.

Getting Ready

Food: Ice pops

Materials: Scissors; napkins; old crayons; white paper; construction paper; pencil sharpeners; wax paper; iron; stapler; paper towels; yarn; illustration of a rainbow; collection box

For this activity you will need old crayons. Sort through your church's crayon boxes and pick out crayons that are broken or worn down. The kids will color Rainbow Reminders with the crayons, and then the crayons will be shaved and melted to create Rainbow Suncatchers.

The Rainbow Reminders will be sent home as reminders that your group is collecting new boxes of crayons for a local shelter. You may also want to say a word to parents, and perhaps put a notice in the church newsletter or bulletin, asking for donations from the rest of the congregation. Decide where the donated crayons will go. Almost any shelter or relief agency will welcome the donation.

Make a sample Rainbow Suncatcher. Cut a piece of construction paper in half horizontally. Fold one of the halves and cut a frame. Cut two wax paper squares the size of the frame. Using a hand-held pencil sharpener, shave a variety of colors onto a wax paper square. Cover it with another square. Iron until the wax melts. Staple the frame to the wax paper; staple a loop of yarn to the top. It's best to cut the wax paper squares, frames, and loops of yarn ahead of time.

If you can't locate an illustration of a rainbow, draw your own with the colors in this order, starting from the top of the arc: red, orange, yellow, green, blue, violet.

Just before the kids arrive, arrange freezer pops (the variety that come sealed in plastic) in a fan shape. Have scissors nearby for snipping off ends and napkins to keep hands from getting too cold.

Sharing God's Colors

Say: **Please take a pop from our rainbow of pops.**
Talk to the kids as they enjoy their snack.
Say: **Today we're going to talk about God's gift of color.**
Lead the kids in a color prayer.
Pray: **Dear God, for red and yellow, blue and green, and all the colors in between, we thank you. Amen.**

Next, ask the kids if they have ever seen a rainbow, then have them tell their rainbow stories. Say: **We don't see rainbows very often, but when we do, what a magnificent sight.**

Ask: **Can anyone tell me about the most famous rainbow in history?** (*the rainbow after the flood*)

Read Genesis 9:13, commenting that Noah and his family must have been delighted to see a beautiful rainbow after so much rain.

Say: **A rainbow is an arc of color that appears in the sky when the sun shines after rain. The raindrops work as prisms that break up the sunlight into the colors of the spectrum. The colors in a rainbow are always in the same order: red, orange, yellow, green, blue, violet. Here's a clever saying to help you remember the order of the colors: "Rainbow Over Yonder, God's Blessing in View." Show kids the illustration of a rainbow, explaining that sometimes the colors may appear to run together, but they are always in this order.**

Next, tell kids about the crayon drive, explaining where the boxes of crayons they donate will go and reminding them how much fun a brand new box of crayons is to use. Show them the assortment of old crayons.

Say: **These have been good crayons but they have seen better days. In just a few minutes we're going to use them to make something new, but first, let's color with them one last time.**

Have the kids color Rainbow Reminders. Tell them to create rainbows with the colors in the correct order, using the saying as a guide. Then have them write the word *crayons* in bright colors.

Next, explain to the kids that since the sun catches raindrops to make rainbows, they are going to use the old crayons to make Rainbow Suncatchers. Give them each a piece of paper towel to put under a wax paper square. Show them how to use the pencil sharpeners to create crayon shavings on the wax paper. Older kids may enjoy trying to arrange their shavings in the order of the rainbow. Then have the kids put another piece of wax paper on top. Carefully take the hot iron and iron each child's creation. Finally, have kids staple the frame over the wax paper and staple a loop of yarn at the top.

Rainbows and crayons— God has created a colorful world.

PINE CONE TREATS
OUR CHURCHYARD BIRDS

Kids will make a treat for themselves and a different treat for the birds.

Psalm 84:3

Even the sparrow finds a home, and the swallow a nest for herself, where she may lay her young, at your altars, O LORD of hosts, my King and my God.

Getting Ready

Food: Churchyard Nests; jellybeans or small oval candies; peanut butter; butter or cookie spray for greasing hands

Materials: Pine cones; birdseed; yarn; scissors; newspaper; knives; large spoon; pan; large pot; wax paper; Bible

Recipe for Churchyard Nests: 6 cups cocoa-flavored rice cereal; 1 package (10 ounces) marshmallows; 4 tablespoons butter or margarine.

Melt butter in a large pot over low heat. Add marshmallows and stir until melted. Remove from heat, add the cereal, and stir.

You may want to recruit a helper to begin to melt the butter and marshmallows for the Churchyard Nests while you take the kids outside to hang their Pine Cone Treats.

Kids will create Pine Cone Treats for the birds in your churchyard. You will need one medium or large pine cone per child. Scout about your churchyard, looking for a tree with low branches where kids can hang their finished Pine Cone Treats. Birds will be more likely to visit the tree if it isn't too near the building. If you don't have a suitable tree in your churchyard or nearby, you can send the Pine Cone Treats home with the kids, encouraging them to find a suitable tree.

Before kids arrive, cover the table with newspaper. Pour the birdseed into a pan, placing it on the table along with the peanut butter, knives, scissors, and yarn.

Sharing Treats With the Birds

Begin by giving kids some information about birds in the Bible.

Say: **Birds are mentioned throughout the Bible, beginning with the story of Creation in Genesis. Sea gulls, doves, ravens, storks, hens, owls, sparrows, swallows, and eagles are among the birds mentioned in the Bible by name. In Bible times, bats, which we now know are mammals, were thought to be birds.**

Continue: **Birds play an important role in several Bible stories. Noah first sends a raven out of the ark to see if the flood waters have gone down, then he sends a dove** (*Genesis 8:6-12*). **At the baptism of Jesus, the Holy Spirit descends in the form of a dove** (*Luke 3:22*). **And although the Bible tells us that humans are more important than birds, God wants us to respect them as creatures of his wonderful creation. Listen to what this line from Psalm 84 says about birds.**

Read Psalm 84:3.

Say: **This verse talks of the birds that nest near the temple.**

Ask: **Have any of you ever seen or heard birds in our churchyard?**

Say: **Today we're going to make a treat for the birds who nest near our church. Afterwards we will make a treat for ourselves too.**

Demonstrate how to coat the pine cone with peanut butter, then roll it in the birdseed. Shake off the birdseed into the pan, then tie a length of yarn around the pine cone to create a hanger.

Lead kids outside with their Pine Cone Treats. Have them keep a lookout for any birds they see. Gather around the branches near the chosen tree and ask the kids to bow their heads.

Pray: **God of the sparrow and the dove, the robin and the eagle, bless these treats to the nourishment of the birds who live near our church. Amen.**

Then have kids tie their Pine Cone Treats to a tree branch.

When you return, ask kids to be seated. Give them each a sheet of wax paper and set out the candy eggs. After the mixture has been prepared for the Churchyard Nests, have kids grease their hands. Give them each about a half cup of the mixture. Show them how to fashion the mixture into the shape of a bird's nest, using their thumbs to make an indentation in the center. When the nests are shaped, they are to put several candy eggs in the center.

How many different kinds of birds can you identify?

Admire the Churchyard Nests before inviting kids to enjoy them as their snack.

TRAY FAVORS
GREETING WITH HOLY KISSES

Make tray favors that are sealed with a kiss, then enjoy cookies topped with Hershey's Kisses candy.

Romans 16:16

Greet one another with a holy kiss.

Getting Ready

Foods: Ready-to-bake cookie dough; Hershey's Kisses

Materials: Small envelopes; crayons or markers; baking sheets; knife; spatula; Bible (optional; rubber stamp, embosser, or seals)

You will need three Kisses per tray favor, one for each child upon arrival, and one to top every cookie. There are about eighty kisses in a bag.

Decide where you will donate the finished tray favors. Hospitals, nursing homes, shelters, and Meals on Wheels often welcome tray favors to add a bit of cheer to a meal. Since some patients have dietary restrictions, do mention that there are Hershey's Kisses in the favors.

Make a sample tray favor. Decorate an envelope with the letters "SWAK," which stands for "sealed with a kiss" and "X's and "O's to represent hugs and kisses. If your church has a rubber stamp, embosser, or seals, you may want to mark the envelopes with your church's name ahead of time or have the kids do this. Place three Kisses inside the envelope and seal.

Place a Kiss on each cookie, then bake the cookies according to the directions on the package. If it isn't practical to have the kids bake the cookies at church, do this ahead of time.

Sharing Holy Kisses

As kids arrive, hand them each a candy Kiss.

Say: A Kiss for you. (*They may eat the Kiss.*)

Have the kids sit down.

Say: I gave you each a Kiss to greet you when you came in. In Bible days people often greeted each other with real kisses just as we do today. Since the early Christians exchanged kisses upon greeting, these kisses became a sign of Christian love.

Read Romans 16:16. Ask the kids to then repeat the verse after you.

Say: Paul wrote this letter to the church in Rome. Sometimes when we seal a letter, we write on the outside "SWAK," which stands for "sealed with a kiss." We're going to show our Christian love by sealing envelopes with Hershey's Kisses to make tray favors.

Explain where the tray favors will go and show kids the sample. Bring out the Kisses, envelopes, and markers or crayons.

While the kids work, call them over a few at a time to put cookies on the baking sheet and a Kiss on top of each cookie. When the cookies are decorated, put them in the oven to bake.

These candy treats are sealed with a kiss.

Pray: Dear God, we sealed our tray favors with Kisses. May they bring the love and joy of a holy kiss to those who receive them. Amen.

After the cookies are finished, give them to the kids.

Say: More Kisses for you.

A MIXER
ENTERTAINING ANGELS

Entertaining another group is fun with the Mingling Angels Game and a heavenly treat of Angelcakes.

Hebrews 13:2

Do not neglect to show hospitality to strangers, for by doing that some have entertained angels without knowing it.

Getting Ready

Food: Angel food cake; fresh or frozen fruit or fruit toppings; canned whipping cream

Materials: Plates; forks; bowls; markers; white paper; stapler, serrated knife; Bible (optional: nametags)

This activity is designed to help introduce two groups to each other though a game, snack, and fellowship. Consider inviting a group from another church. If this isn't't practical, you may invite another group from your own church. Don't overlook adults, who might especially appreciate this opportunity to get to know your kids better.

Everyone will wear paper halos during the Mingling Angels Game. Create lengths of paper measuring about two by twenty-four inches by stapling two strips together. Strips will be adjusted and stapled to fit heads as everyone arrives.

During the game players will ask questions to determine what is written on their halo. Younger kids will have fun guessing the names of animals. For older kids you may want to use Christian symbols. Here are some suggested symbols: cross, ship, fish, bread, coin, rainbow, angel, grape, butterfly, candle, triangle, star, dove, heart, and lamb. You can either draw or write the name of the animal or symbol on the middle of the paper strip. If you have a large group, you may need to repeat animals or symbols. Place strips in a box or bag to keep them out of view.

Purchase or bake angel food cake. The cake will be sliced, topped with fruit, and garnished with whipping cream to create Angelcakes. A large angel food cake will yield about twelve slices. Slice the cake ahead of time with a serrated knife and place the fruit in bowls.

Sharing a Game, Angelcakes, and Fellowship

As your kids and the guests arrive, welcome them and have them don nametags, if you have decided to use them. Then fit a halo on each head, being careful not to reveal the animal or symbol to the wearer. Caution each person not to tell anyone else what is on his or her halo, either.

Gather kids and guests together.

Say: Welcome! (*Explain to your kids who their guests are.*) **Since you are all wearing halos, you must be angels. To help you get to know one another, we are going to begin by playing the Mingling Angels Game.**

Explain that all angels are to circulate around the room, introducing themselves and asking questions to try and determine what is on their halos. Tell the group that the halos have animals/Christian symbols on them. They are to ask only yes and no questions until they have figured out what their animal or symbol is. For example, for the animals they might ask: "Does it hop? Is it green?" For symbols: "Is it a food? Is it in the sky?"

When all have guessed what is on their halos, call them back together.

Say: I hope that you don't feel like strangers to one another anymore after playing the Mingling Angels Game. I turned you into angels today so that you could get to know one another better, but also in honor of a verse in the Bible.

Read Hebrews 13:2.

Say: We are showing our guests hospitality today. We invited you and we are so glad that you are here! Sometimes as Christians we are called to show hospitality to people we don't even know.

Ask: Can anyone give me an example of a time when you have showed hospitality to someone you didn't really know? (*I gave a boy my leftover ride tickets at the fair; I helped a lady in the store who spilled her purse; my mom and I volunteered at the food pantry.*)

Say: All of us, especially kids, need to be careful about strangers, but as Christians, there are times when we can be helpful and kind to people we don't even know.

Ask everyone to join hands for prayer.

Pray: God of All, we thank you for this chance to mingle today and to get to know one another. As Christians help us show hospitality and love to everyone.

Say: In honor of our guests and our game and our Bible verse, we're serving Angelcakes today.

Let your kids help you serve the guests before helping themselves. And of course, as the dessert is enjoyed, encourage your kids and the guests to continue mingling with one another.

I was a stranger, and you welcomed me.

DISASTER RELIEF
COLLECTING PLATES AND SUCH

Fashioning Platemobiles and PB and J Sandwiches sparks a project to collect disposable dinnerware for disaster relief.

John 21:15

When they had finished breakfast, Jesus said to Simon Peter, "Simon, son of John, do you love me more than these?" He said to him, "Yes, Lord, you know that I love you." Jesus said to him, "Feed my lambs."

Getting Ready

Food: Peanut butter; jelly; sliced bread; milk

Materials: Bible; white paper plates; paper cups; plastic knives, forks, and spoons; yarn; tape; paper punch; scissors; crayons or markers; collection box

Kids will make Platemobiles as a collection reminder, using plates, cups, and utensils. Plan on making several extra mobiles to hang around the church.

Precut yarn in these lengths for each mobile: one 12-inch, two 18-inch, and one 24-inch. Also punch a hole through the bottom of one cup for each mobile.

You may want to set up a collection basket or box at church and put a notice in your bulletin and/or newsletter explaining the project. In most communities there are relief organizations that welcome donations of disposable dinnerware.

Kids will make their own PB and J Sandwiches for the snack and enjoy them along with a cup of milk

Sharing Paper Plates and Such

Begin by asking kids to recall disasters that have happened to people and groups in their community, county, or state (ice storms, fires, tornadoes, earthquakes, hurricanes).

Say: In disasters our normal way of life is disrupted. We may have no power or water or dishes left to use. People may be camped out, staying in shelters, or packed into the homes of friends or family. In such times there are many things that the disaster victims need. One of these things is food and another is plates, cups, and utensils to use when they eat. We can help our community to be ready to assist disaster victims by collecting paper plates, cups, and plastic utensils. Today, we'll make Platemobiles with these items and use them as reminders in our homes and around our church. But first we'll fix a staple food of disaster relief—peanut butter and jelly sandwiches, also fondly known as PB and J Sandwiches.

When the kids have prepared their snack, invite them to begin eating. Read John 21:12-17.

Ask: What single question does Jesus keep asking Simon Peter? (*Do you love me?*) **When our parents or teachers ask us a single question over and over, why do they do it?** (*to get our attention; to let us know the question is important; to see if we change our answers*) **Did Jesus have Peter's attention?** (*yes*) **Did**

Peter know this was an important question? (*Maybe, but he was hurt to be asked a third time.*) **Did Peter change his answer?** (*No, he always said that he loved Jesus.*) **What did Jesus want Peter to do?** (*feed and tend his sheep*) **Who do you think Jesus' sheep are?** (*his believers*)

Say: Jesus charged Peter to take care of people in the early church and this same message speaks to us today. If we love Jesus then we too must feed and care for his believers.

Pray: Dear God, we love Jesus and want to tend his sheep. Let us be his helpers in this world. Amen.

Tell the kids that now it's time to make Platemobiles. Have them begin by printing: "Please donate these by (*date*)." Assist younger kids. Plates may be further embellished by adding "Feed My Sheep" along with drawings of sheep or by writing "Disaster Relief," along with pictures of flame, rain, tornadoes, and so forth.

Next, each plate will need four holes. The first hole is center top for the hanger; the second is center bottom; the third is two inches left of center bottom; and the fourth is two inches right of center bottom.

Next comes the yarn. Give each child a 12-inch length to loop and knot as a hanger in the center top hole. Then tie the 24-inch length to the center bottom hole. Finally tie the two 18-inch lengths to the holes on either side of the center bottom.

At the end of one 18-inch length, have kids tape the handle of the plastic fork so that it will dangle and swing freely. On the other 18-inch length, do the same with the plastic spoon.

To complete the mobile have kids thread the 24-inch length of yarn through the cup, with the cup upside down, resembling a bell. Tell everyone to push the cups along the yarn until the cup is next to the plate. About halfway along the length of yarn, fold a two-inch strip of tape around the yarn to create a stop for the cup. Slide the cup down the yarn gently to meet the stop. Finish by taping the handle of a plastic knife on the end of the piece of yarn.

Explain to kids that they are to hang their mobiles at home as reminders to purchase and bring in the disposable dinnerware. Hang a few Platemobiles around the church too.

May the wind of the Holy Spirit move your mobiles and your church to contribute to this project.

COOKIE BAKING AND DELIVERY
THANKING COMMUNITY HELPERS

Naming our community helpers and pantomiming their work helps us understand what they do, and baking them cookies gives us a delicious way to show our heartfelt appreciation.

1 Corinthians 10:31

So, whether you eat or drink, or whatever you do, do everything for the glory of God.

Getting Ready

Food: Cookie dough; milk

Materials: Baking sheets; spatula; timer; knives (for slice-and-bake cookies) or spoons (for batter cookies); two disposable plates; plastic wrap; cups; index cards; markers or crayons; Bible

You will need two generous batches of homemade cookie dough or enough ready-made cookie dough to yield eight dozen cookies. Two plates of thirty cookies each will be prepared for community helpers, and you will want kids to have at least two cookies apiece for the snack.

Decide if it is best for you to select the two community organizations who will receive the cookies (for ease and timing of delivery) or whether the kids will choose.

Sharing Cookies

Say: **Listen to what Paul wrote to the Corinthians.**
Read 1 Corinthians 10:31.
Say: **When we think of the things that are done for the glory of God, we often think of good deeds done by good people.**
Ask: **Can you name some people who help our community?**
(firefighters; pastors; the rescue squad; librarians; public safety officers)
Say: **These hardworking community helpers are people we can turn to when we need assistance. Let's show them our gratitude for their hard work by doing something nice. Let's bake cookies for them!**
Preheat the oven while the kids slice or spoon the cookie dough onto baking sheets. Remember to set a timer so that you can play a pantomime game while the cookies are baking.

To play the pantomime game ask groups of two or three kids to silently act out a scene portraying community helpers at work. (Ideas: firemen putting out a house fire; Red Cross nurse taking blood; a policewoman helping at the scene of an accident; food bank workers filling bags with groceries; Habitat for Humanity helpers building a house)

When the baking is finished, fill the gift plates and cover them with plastic wrap.

Offer a prayer before kids enjoy their cookies and milk.

Pray: God of All Good Things, you have blessed us with many community helpers. We thank you for each of them and the work that they do. We thank you too for the warm cookies we are about to taste. We pray that whatever we eat or drink or whatever we do, we'll do everything in your glory. Amen.

Finally, ask kids to use the index cards and markers or crayons to write thank-you notes and to sign their names. Deliver these personal notes along with the freshly baked cookies to your deserving community helpers.

Help yourself to cookies! You're a community helper too.

DECORATING WATER BOTTLES
WATER AS A GIFT

Discussing our thirst and pretending to run in a marathon readies us to give a gift of water and to enjoy a drink too!

Revelation 21:6

I am the Alpha and the Omega, the beginning and the end. To the thirsty I will give water as a gift from the spring of the water of life.

Getting Ready

Food: Powdered drink mix; commercially packaged bottles of water

Materials: Bible; blank adhesive package labels; crayons and/or ball-point pens; cups; spoons

Decide who will receive the decorated water bottles. Those participating in Crop Walk, running a charity 5K marathon, laboring at a

Habitat House, or helping with a church workday will appreciate the gift. Buyer's clubs sell bottled water by the case at reasonable prices. Most food stores also have bottled water for sale.

The powdered drink mix will help quench the thirst of your own group.

Sharing a Gift of Water

Begin by asking kids to tell some of their favorite ways to play in water. (*rafting; splashing in a water park; swimming; fishing; running in a sprinkler*)

Say: **Playing in the water brings us hours of fun, but when we play or exercise, we need to drink water too. Our bodies must have water in order to be healthy. The body lets us know if we need water by making us feel thirsty.**

Ask: **What activities make you feel thirsty?** (*bicycling; soccer; basketball*)

Say: **I know of some people who are going to feel very thirsty when they** (*walk/run/work*) **for** (*charity/organization*)**. We're going to give them water bottles that we have decorated. Our gift will lift their spirits and quench their thirst.**

To decorate bottles, give kids lots of labels to color with drawings of water sports, water scenes, or water-related activities. If you have some who would rather write than color, they may print: "To the thirsty I will give water as a gift" (Revelation 21:6). As kids finish the labels, have them stick them on the bottles. If you have extra labels, let kids put several labels on some of the bottles.

Next read Revelation 21:6.

Say: **God has given us earthly water for our bodies and spiritual water for our souls. We get spiritual water from praying, reading the Bible, going to worship, talking about our faith, and sharing fellowship with other believers.**

Next, play a new version of "Going on a Bear Hunt." Kids may sit or stand. Instruct them to step in place (or clap hands) and repeat each phrase after you.

Say: **Going to a marathon . . . going to run a race . . . can't wear sandals . . . got to wear running shoes . . . can't be shy . . . got to sign in . . . can't stand still . . . got to warm up . . . time to line up . . . time to go, go, go . . . can't run slow . . . got to run fast . . . can't go backward . . . got to go forward . . . got to run uphill . . . got to run downhill . . . got to turn left . . . got to turn right . . . can't twist my ankle . . . got to be strong . . . can't be distracted . . . got to stay focused . . . need to pass a runner . . . feeling kind of tired . . . can't slow down . . . feeling really** thirsty . . . can't get dehydrated . . . got to grab some water . . . thank you, volunteers . . . sure like these labels . . . now I feel better . . . can't quit now . . . got to keep running . . . step by step . . . mile by mile . . . got to keep going . . . hear the crowd cheering . . . see the finish line shining . . . can't wait to cross it . . . I ran the race . . . feeling so happy . . . can't believe it's over . . . want to run again . . . be there next week . . . going to run a marathon.

Now ask the kids to bow their heads.

Pray: God of the Beginning and God of the End, we thank you for being with us at the beginning and end of our races, our days, and our lives. Quench our thirsty bodies and souls with your gift of water and bless our gifts of bottled water. In Jesus' name. Amen.

Say thank you for God's gift of water.

Invite the kids to make drinks using the powdered mix and water.

ZIP-UP SNACKS
TREATS To SHARE

Zip up a cereal snack for kids in a younger class to remind one and all of Jesus' love.

Matthew 19:14

But Jesus said, "Let the children come to me, and do not stop them; for it is to such as these that the kingdom of heaven belongs."

Getting Ready

Food: A box of a sweet, puffed cereal and a box of an oat ring or rice squares cereal

Materials: Snack-sized reclosable food storage bags; two mixing bowls; large spoons

Select cereals that will have a compatible taste when combined. Avoid flake or granola cereals since they will be too messy for little fingers. Your group will mix the cereals and bag them as a surprise for a younger group at church. Make arrangements with the teacher, explaining the project and giving the date that your kids will bring the younger kids Zip-Up Snacks.

Sharing Zip-Up Snacks

Begin by singing "Jesus Loves Me":

> Jesus loves me! This I know,
> for the Bible tells me so.
> Little ones to him belong;
> they are weak, but he is strong.
> Yes, Jesus loves me! Yes, Jesus loves me!
> Yes, Jesus loves me! The Bible tells me so.
>
> Jesus loves me! This I know,
> as he loved so long ago,
> taking children on his knee,
> saying, "Let them come to me."
> Yes, Jesus loves me! Yes, Jesus loves me!
> Yes, Jesus loves me! The Bible tells me so.

Stanza 1: Anna B. Warner, 1860; stanza 2: David Rutherford McGuire, 1962.

Say: In this song we sing that we know Jesus loves us because the Bible tells us so. One of the passages in the Bible that tells of the love of Jesus is in the Book of Matthew.
Read Matthew 19:13-15.

Ask: Who wanted to keep the children away from Jesus? (*the disciples*) **Do you have any ideas about why the disciples thought they should do this?** (*Children weren't considered as important as adults; they thought Jesus was too busy.*) **What did Jesus say to let everyone know that children are important?** (*The kingdom of heaven belongs to them.*)

Say: Jesus showed his love for children and proclaimed their importance to the disciples. The words he spoke on that day so long ago are true today: Jesus loves you and to you belongs the kingdom of heaven. This is a valuable message for us to share with younger kids.

Explain to your kids who they will surprise with the treat they are about to create, Zip-Up Snacks.

Divide the group according to tasks: pouring cereal, mixing, scooping, bag holding, and bag sealing.

To make the Zip-Up Snacks, pour half of both boxes of cereal into each of the two bowls. Mix, then begin the scooping and bagging process. When the treat is bagged and zipped, kids may take a bag for themselves.

Pray: Gracious Lord, thank you for your love and care. We will proclaim your blessing to other children, so they may rejoice along with us. Amen.

When the snack is finished, visit the class of younger kids, presenting your church-made treats and singing "Jesus Loves Me!"

God loves it when God's children sing.

SAUCY SURPRISES
HELP FOR HOLIDAY MEALS

Since food delivery agencies need extra help during the holidays, decorate applesauce cups as gifts and learn that helping others is also helping Jesus.

Matthew 25:40

And the king will answer them, "Truly I tell you, just as you did it to one of the least of these who are members of my family, you did it to me."

Getting Ready

Food: A variety of single-serving applesauce cups in different flavors; raisins, cinnamon red hots, and sprinkles

Materials: Bible; a large bag of stick-on gift bows; several sheets of gummed foil stars; spoons; bowls; box for delivery

Over the holidays, organizations such as Meals on Wheels need ready-to-eat, single-serving foods to leave with their clients on the days when there is no delivery or food preparation. Check with your local Meals on Wheels, food bank, or shelter to find out how many cups they might use over a holiday. Purchase applesauce cups accordingly. Be sure to include one cup per child for your group's snack. Kids will stir in raisins, red hots, and/or sprinkles. Place stir-ins into bowls.

Sharing Saucy Surprises

Begin by holding up a bow.

Ask: **What do you think of when you see a bow?** (*a gift*) **How does receiving a gift usually make you feel?** (*happy; excited; surprised*) **Can you remember a time when you felt happy to give a gift?** (*I gave my brother a toy he really wanted; I gave my grandmother some slippers she said she needed.*)

Say: **Sometimes it's a lot of fun to give a gift that is playful, silly, or fancy, but other times it's better to give a gift that someone truly needs.**

Read Matthew 25:35-40.

Say: **In this passage Jesus used the story of a king to explain that when we help people in need, we are helping him. This means that if we want to give Jesus our love, we can do so by helping others. We're going to decorate Saucy Surprises as gifts for people who are hungry, sick, and older.**

Show the applesauce cups, bows, and stars to the kids. Demonstrate the decoration by pressing a few stars around the outside of the cup, then sticking a bow on top. Invite the kids to do the same. While they work, tell them about the mission of the organization you are helping. The Meals on Wheels program brings one meal each weekday to those on its list. During the meal delivery volunteers visit and check on people. Explain that over holidays the organization needs to make special plans. Since meals aren't usually delivered on those days, your Saucy Surprises will help.

When the project is completed, admire the fine and fancy decorations.

Say: **You have certainly made these Saucy Surprises look like delightful gifts that will surprise those who receive them!**

Ask everyone to hold a decorated cup and to stand in a circle for a prayer. Have kids repeat the following prayer after you, one line at a time.

Pray: **Giving is great . . . giving is good . . . now we give a gift of food . . . by our hands, others are fed . . . we thank you, Lord, for applesauce and daily bread. Amen.**

Carefully stack Saucy Surprises into the box for delivery, then surprise your kids with stir-ins for their own applesauce cups.

Good things come in little packages!

SAMPLING FOODS OF THE HOLY LAND

BOWL BREAD
BACK TO BIBLE TIMES

Bake bread over a bowl just as it was done so many years ago.

Matthew 6:11

Give us this day our daily bread.

Getting Ready

Food: Canned crescent rolls; cooking oil or cooking spray

Materials: A large oven-proof bowl

Kids will help place the crescent roll dough over an inverted bowl. The bowl will then be put into an oven preheated to 375 degrees until the dough is lightly browned (about ten or fifteen minutes.) If you have a large group, you may want to prepare two or more loaves of bowl bread.

Sampling Bowl Bread

Begin by leading kids in the Lord's Prayer:
Our Father, who art in heaven,
hallowed be thy name,
Thy kingdom come,
thy will be done on earth as it is in heaven.
Give us this day our daily bread.
And forgive us our trespasses,
    as we forgive those who trespass against us.
        And lead us not into temptation,
            but deliver us from evil.
                For thine is the kingdom, and the power,
                and the glory, forever. Amen.

From The Ritual of the Former Methodist Church, *The United Methodist Hymnal,* © 1989 The United Methodist Publishing House; 895.

84

Ask: What food is mentioned in the Lord's Prayer? (*bread*)

Say: Raise your hand if you eat bread just about every day. Let the kids respond.

Say: In the Lord's Prayer daily bread can really mean the food that we need to nourish our bodies. Some people eat bread every day, some don't, but we all need food for nourishment. When we pray the Lord's Prayer, we ask God for this food.

Continue: In Bible times, just as today, people ate lots of bread. Since they didn't have food stores or bakeries, they had to bake their own almost every day. The bread was usually made with wheat or barley flour. It was mixed in a bowl, patted into a flat circle, and then baked on a hot stone or over a bowl.

Tell the kids you are going to make Bowl Bread, with a few modern shortcuts. Have someone grease a bowl using cooking spray or a small amount of oil. Tear apart the crescent roll dough. Have kids lay the dough over the bowl. Each piece should overlap the next slightly, forming a cap over the top of the bowl. Gently press edges together. Place the bowl carefully into the preheated oven.

While the bread is baking, encourage kids to share what sort of bread they like, what spreads they enjoy putting on their bread, and any experiences they have had with bread baking.

When the bread is done, let it cool for a few minutes before you take it off the bowl. If you are careful, you should be able to remove the bread so that it is in one piece and keeps its rounded shape.. Don't worry if it breaks, the flavor will still be wonderful. Let kids tear off pieces and enjoy.

Remember, you cannot live by bread alone.

PISTACHIO NUTS AND ALMONDS
CHOICE FRUITS OF THE LAND

Fill a paper bag with pictures of your very favorite foods before opening a small cloth bag containing two favorite foods from long ago.

Genesis 43:11

Then their father Israel said to them, "If it must be so, then do this: take some of the choice fruits of the land in your bags, and carry them down as a present to the man—a little balm and a little honey, gum, resin, pistachio nuts, and almonds."

Getting Ready

Food: Pistachio nuts (shelled or unshelled); almonds (shelled)

Materials: Paper bags; magazines; scissors; cotton fabric; yarn or string; Bible

Kids will cut pictures from magazines of their favorite foods, then place the pictures into the paper bags. To simplify the project for younger kids, you may want to tear out magazine pages ahead of time. The kids can then choose the ones they want and trim around them.

Cut the fabric into six-inch squares. Put about one-third cup of the nuts inside each square and tie with lengths of string or yarn. Keep the fabric bags out of sight as kids arrive.

Sampling Pistachio Nuts and Almonds

Say: **We are going to pretend to pack bags of our favorite foods to give as gifts.**

Hand each kid a paper bag and ask each one to find pictures of his or her favorite foods to put inside it. When all of the kids have found at least four or five pictures to put in their bags, have them get into groups of two or three. Ask them to share the contents of their bags with one another by showing the pictures and saying a word or two about each favorite food.

Call the kids back together and ask them to stand in a circle. Explain that you will say the opening words of a prayer, then each person will name a favorite food. Indicate who will begin and in what direction the prayer will move around the circle.

Pray: **Dear God, we are grateful for all of the wonderful foods you have given us. Here are some of our very favorites.** (*The kids will each say a favorite, then you will add your own.*) **Thank you for food and for all your good gifts, sent to us from heaven above. Amen.**

Tell the kids that in Bible times, people had favorite foods too. Hand each child a fabric bag, with instructions that the bag not be opened yet.

Read Genesis 43:11, explaining that in the story of Joseph, these were some of the foods considered to be choice fruits of the land. Joseph's father instructed his sons to pack the foods into a bag to take as a gift.

Invite kids to open their cloth bags, having them identify the pistachio nuts and the almonds. As they sample the nuts, give them a bit of Biblical background.

Say: Both pistachio nuts and almonds grew in Bible times and are still enjoyed in the Holy Land today. The word for *almond* in Hebrew means "awakening one," most likely because the almond tree is the first tree to awaken in the spring. The trees flower with pink blossoms in January. The pistachio tree is also called a "green almond," because the nuts are greenish in color. Today our pistachios are sometimes dyed red. Both pistachio nuts and almonds are used in candies and can be pressed into oil. Of course, they are quite delicious eaten just as you are eating them right now!

Are you nuts over nuts? What kinds?

CAROB
BEAN POD OR BUG?

After questioning what John the Baptist really ate in the wilderness, savor a carob-covered treat.

Mark 1:6

Now John was clothed with camel's hair, with a leather belt around his waist, and he ate locusts and wild honey.

Getting Ready

Food: Carob-covered candy

Materials: Bible; bowl; photograph or drawing of locust, the carob tree, and locust, the insect

This activity raises the question: Did John the Baptist eat the pods of the locust tree or an insect, the locust, while living in the wilderness?

Kids will enjoy looking at pictures of the insect and tree, which you should be able to locate in an encyclopedia or Bible reference book. The locust is similar in appearance to the grasshopper or the cricket, if you can't find a picture of an actual locust.

Carob-covered candy is available in most health food and candy stores and some food stores. If you can[t locate carob, chocolate has a similar flavor and can be substituted. Place the candy in a bowl.

Sampling the Locust

Gather the kids together. Hold up the picture of the insect, if you have one.

Ask: Would you like to eat this? (*no*)

If you don't have a picture, simply ask: **How many of you would like to eat a locust, cricket, or grasshopper?**

Next, hold up the carob-covered candy.

Ask: Would you like to eat this? (*yes*)

Say: The first food I showed you was a locust (or insect that is similar to a locust). In Bible times, people ate locusts. The insects were roasted lightly, dried in the sun, and then salted. The wings, legs, head, and intestines were usually removed before the locust was eaten.

Continue: The second food I showed you was candy with a carob coating. The carob tree is also called the locust tree. This tree, which grows in the Holy Land, bears large bean like pods that can be eaten. (*Show kids the picture of the locust tree, if you have found one.*) **Carob powder is made from these pods and is a delicious flavoring for treats such as these.**

Ask: Can anyone tell me who John the Baptist was? (*He was a messenger who announced the coming of Jesus.*)

Read Mark 1:1-8.

Say: John called people to repent their sins and he baptized many of them in the River Jordan. The Bible tells us that John came from the wilderness, where he ate locusts and wild honey. But what the Bible doesn't tell us is which locust: the insect or the pod? Some Biblical scholars say he ate the insect. Some say he ate the pod. Some say he ate both.

With a smile, announce that you have decided your group would rather eat candy made from locust pods than a real bug.

Before you serve the candy, ask the kids to bow their heads.

Pray: Dear God, we thank you for John the Baptist, who told the people that Jesus was coming, and we thank you for this treat. Amen.

Brave enough to eat a bug?

LENTILS
THE SoP

After hearing one of the most famous food stories in the Bible, scoop up lentil stew just as Esau did.

Genesis 25:34

Then Jacob gave Esau bread and lentil stew, and he ate and drank, and rose and went his way. Thus Esau despised his birthright.

Getting Ready

Food: Lentil soup; pita bread

Materials: Bible; serving bowl; basket; knife

Kids will dip pita bread into the soup from a group bowl, just as people did in Bible times. Depending on the size of your group, you may want to use several bowls. One can of soup per bowl should be enough. Slice the round pita bread into pie-shaped wedges large enough for dipping. Place the wedges in a basket.

Just before kids arrive, heat the lentil soup, draining off some of the liquid.

Sampling Lentils

Set out the foods and invite the kids to gather round.

Say: **This is lentil soup. It plays a role in one of the most important food stories in the Bible, a story about the twins, Jacob and Esau. Because Esau was born first, he was considered the older of the twins and therefore was entitled to the birthright. This meant that he would inherit more of the family property and that he would succeed his father as head of the family. In Bible days you could sell your birthright to a younger brother. Listen to learn what Esau sold his birthright for.**

Read Genesis 25:29-34.

Ask: **What did Esau sell his birthright for?** (*bread and lentil stew*)

Say: **Not many people would sell their birthright for a bowl of lentil stew, but in Bible days this was a popular food, and Esau was really hungry. The lentil is a plant that grows in the Holy Land. Its seeds are nutritious, providing both protein and carbohydrates.**

Ask: **Have any of you tried lentils?** (*Let the kids respond.*)

Say: **For those who haven't ever eaten lentils, today is your chance! And we are going to eat the stew just as Esau and others** did in Bible days. Stews and many other foods were scooped up with a piece of bread since forks and spoons were not common. This was called "the sop." The master of the feast would sometimes dip guests' bread for them as a sign of hospitality. He would then hand the dipped bread to the guests. I'm going to hand each of you a piece of bread but let you dip it in the stew yourself, so you can have the fun of sopping it up.

Hand the bread to the kids, asking them to hold it.

Pray: Dear God, it's fun to remember the stories and foods and traditions of Bible times. Thank you for this stew and for this bread. Amen.

Encourage kids not to dip the same piece of bread back into the stew, reminding them that we are more germ-conscious than folks were in Bible days.

Hey, in Bible times at least there weren't many dishes to wash!

CINNAMON
THE FINEST OF SPICES

Take in the aroma and flavor of cinnamon while learning about this ancient spice, then make sweet-smelling Cinnamon Sachets.

Exodus 30:22-23

The LORD spoke to Moses: Take the finest spices: of liquid myrrh five hundred shekels, and of sweet-smelling cinnamon half as much, that is, two hundred fifty, and two hundred fifty of aromatic cane.

Getting Ready

Foods: Powdered cinnamon; cinnamon sticks; cinnamon-flavored snack such as cereal or graham crackers

Materials: Bowls; napkin; ribbon; teaspoon; Bible

Wrap a few teaspoons of powdered cinnamon in a napkin and secure with ribbon. This will be passed around for the kids to sniff and then guess what spice is inside.

You may want to bring several snacks flavored with cinnamon, although one is sufficient. Place the snack in bowls.

The kids will tie ribbon about twelve inches long onto cinnamon sticks to make Cinnamon Sachets. You may want to precut the ribbon for younger kids.

Sampling Cinnamon

Begin by passing around the cinnamon wrapped in the napkin. Tell kids that they are each to take a sniff, but not to tell others what they think is inside.

Ask: **What did you smell?** (*cinnamon*)

Say: **In Bible times, cinnamon was used to make anointing oils and perfumes.**

Read Exodus 30:22-23, explaining that in this passage, God is giving Moses instructions for making an anointing oil.

Continue: **Cinnamon was also one of the spices used to put on the bodies of people who had died. Since it had to be purchased from the Near East, it was considered a valuable and important spice. Putting spices on the body of a loved one who had died was a way of showing honor to that person and helped keep the body from having a bad smell.**

Ask: **Does anyone know where cinnamon comes from?** (*from the cinnamon tree*)

Say: **The inner bark of the cinnamon tree is peeled off. It turns brown and curls up as it dries. The bark is then sold as cinnamon sticks or ground into a powder. Hold up the cinnamon stick.**

Continue: **In Bible times, cinnamon was used to add flavor to foods just as it is today.**

Ask the kids to tell you some of their favorite foods flavored with cinnamon.

Pray: **Dear God, thank you for spices such as cinnamon that spice up our lives! Amen.**

Let the kids enjoy the snack.

Say: **In Bible times, cinnamon was used to make clothes or bed linens smell good. Today you're going to use this spice to make Cinnamon Sachets to take home to help your clothes smell good too.**

Demonstrate how to tie the ribbon around the cinnamon stick and finish with a bow.

Three cheers for kids who add spice to life!

OLIVES
AN ANOINTING CEREMONY

Understand how olives were used in Bible times by tasting them and taking part in an anointing ceremony.

Genesis 8:11

And the dove came back to him in the evening, and there in its beak was a freshly plucked olive leaf; so Noah knew that the waters had subsided from the earth.

Getting Ready

Food: Pitted green and black olives; olive oil; bread

Materials: Paper bag; tissues; bowls; basket; plates; Bible

Create a Mystery Bag to introduce the activity by placing three or four olives into a paper bag, then folding the bag closed.

Kids will taste olives and also dip bread into olive oil. A crusty bread such as French will taste best. Place the olives in bowls and break the bread into bite-sized pieces and place it in a basket. A small amount of olive oil will be poured onto the plates just before kids dip their bread. Be certain to keep the foods out of sight until the Mystery Bag has been passed around.

For the anointing ceremony kids will dip their thumbs into a small bowl of oil. Don't pour the olive oil until just before the anointing ceremony begins.

Sampling Olives

Say: There is an important food of the Holy Land in this Mystery Bag. As I pass it around, you are to reach your hand into the bag, touch the food, and try to figure out what it is. Don't peek and don't tell anyone else what you think is in the bag. (*Let everyone have a turn.*)

Say: Now everyone tell me at once, what is in the Mystery Bag? (*olives*)

Bring out the olives, olive oil, and bread. Hold up the bowls of olives, explaining that the green olives are unripened and the black are ripened.

Say: Olive trees grow throughout the Holy Land, sometimes living to be over one thousand years old. In Bible times, olives were served at almost every meal, and there are references to

olives throughout the Bible. Olive leaves even play a role in the story of Noah and the ark.

Read Genesis 8:11.

Say: Olives were eaten, but they had other uses too. They were pressed into oil that was burned in lamps and used in anointing ceremonies. (Hold up the bottle of olive oil.) "To anoint" means "to pour oil upon someone." In Bible times, people were sometimes anointed when they became leaders and sometimes when they were sick. Other times a host would anoint guests as a sign of welcome and friendship. Today, just for fun, you are going to anoint one another with olive oil as a sign of your friendship.

Have each child take a partner. Pour a small amount of olive oil into the bowl. Have partners come forward, one set at a time. One child will dip a thumb into the oil and place it on the other's forehead, saying: I anoint you with olive oil as a sign of friendship. Then the other will do the same. Give kids tissues to wipe off the oil, if they wish. When everyone has had a turn, let a child anoint you too.

Next, announce that it is time to taste olives and olive oil. Ask each child to take just one black and one green olive. If you have extra olives, those who like them can then have more. Encourage everyone to take at least a tiny taste of the olives, reminding kids that in Bible times, children would have eaten lots of olives.

Next, pour a small amount of olive oil onto a plate for each child. Kids are to dip the bread into the oil. Encourage the kids to eat the snack.

Pray: Dear God, we're glad that today we could learn about the ancient olive tree. Amen.

This is a good day to extend an olive branch.

CUCUMBERS
A PICKLE TASTING

A pickle tasting and a cucumber planting celebrate a food the Hebrews missed during those long years in the wilderness.

Numbers 11:5

We remember the fish we used to eat in Egypt for nothing, the cucumbers, the melons, the leeks, the onions, and the garlic.

Getting Ready

Foods: A cucumber; a variety of pickles

Materials: Bible; bowls; sharp knife; fork; cucumber seeds; paper or plastic cups; potting soil; newspaper; spoons

Plan on serving several kinds of pickles such as sweet, dill, Polish, and hot. Kids will appreciate pickles in different shapes and sizes too such as strips, wedges, and gherkins. Fork the pickles into bowls, slicing any that are large into bite-sized pieces. You can use the cucumber just to show to the kids or you can slice one, or several cucumbers to serve along with the pickles.

After the pickle tasting, kids will plant cucumber seeds. Plan on each child planting three seeds per cup. One pack of cucumber seeds should be enough for around ten cups. Since the kids will spoon the planting soil into the cups themselves, it's easiest to put the soil into several bowls. Kids will take the cups home to watch the seeds sprout.

Sampling Cucumbers

Set out the pickles.

Ask: What are these? (*pickles*) **What are these pickles made from?** (*cucumbers*)

Say: These pickles are made from cucumbers. (*Hold up the cucumber.*) **When the Hebrews left Egypt and were traveling in the desert, they missed the delicious cucumbers and other foods that they had eaten in Egypt.**

Read Numbers 11:5.

Say: Cucumbers were cultivated in the gardens of the Holy Land as well as in Egypt. They were considered such an important crop that forts made of leaves were sometimes built near the cucumber crop. Guards hid inside the forts to keep watch for thieves.

Ask: How many of you like cucumbers? How many of you like pickles? (*Let the kids respond.*)

Say: Although pickles are not mentioned in the Bible, pickling is a process that goes back to ancient times. Pickling is an excellent method of preserving food. Salt and vinegar, which are used in pickling, were both readily available in the Holy Land.

Tell the kids that in a moment they will take part in a pickle tasting, but first ask them to bow their heads.

Pray: God of the Garden, we praise you for seeds, and we praise you for gardens, and we praise you for all the good foods that grow on your earth. Amen.

Serve the pickles, encouraging kids to comment on which ones they like and which ones they don't like. Then, tell them that in honor of this Holy Land crop, they are going to plant cucumber seeds.

Spread newspaper on the tables. Kids are to fill the cups halfway with potting soil, place three seeds in the soil, and cover them with another spoonful of soil. When this is done, have them lightly water the seeds.

Explain to the kids that when they take the seeds home, they should keep them in a sunny window or porch, watering them when the soil feels dry. Plants should be thinned once they begin to grow tall. Kids and their families may simply enjoy watching the seeds sprout, or they may want to transfer them to their own gardens.

In a pickle? Pray!

FIGS
LEAVES AND CAKES

Go on a leaf hunt in your own churchyard, then make leaf rubbings and enjoy a figgy snack in honor of figs and their mighty leaves.

1 Chronicles 12:40

And also their neighbors, from as far away as Issachar and Zebulun and Naphtali, came bringing food on donkeys, camels, mules, and oxen—abundant provisions of meal, cakes of figs, clusters of raisins, wine, oil, oxen, and sheep, for there was joy in Israel.

Getting Ready

Food: Figs (in season); fig cookies

Materials: paper; crayons; Bible (optional: fig leaves or illustration of fig leaves)

If figs are in season, kids will enjoy seeing and tasting a fresh fig. If you can locate real fig leaves, bring them along too. If not, look for an illustration of a fig leaf.

For the leaf rubbings, you will need lightweight white paper such as printer or copy paper. If poor weather is imminent, you may want to gather a variety of leaves ahead of time.

Sampling Figs

Ask: **Do you like to help rake leaves? Do you like to jump in leaves?** (*Let the kids respond.*)

Say: Let me tell you about some leaves that were so big that Adam and Eve sewed them together to make clothes in the Garden of Eden (*Genesis 3:7*).

Show the fig leaf or the illustration, if you have one.

Say: Fig leaves are big leaves. Since the leaves are so big, the fig tree provided a nice amount of shade for Bible people. The fruit of the tree, the fig itself, was delicious served fresh, but could also be dried, making it an excellent food for travelers. Dried figs were often pressed into cakes.

Read 1 Chronicles 12:40.

Say: This passage describes the celebration that was held when David became the king. The travelers who came to the celebration brought fig cakes. In honor of fig leaves and all the interesting leaves in God's world, we're going to go on a leaf hunt. When we return, we'll make leaf rubbings and enjoy a snack of fig cakes.

Lead kids outdoors, telling them each to take a leaf from several trees. Once back indoors, have them lay the leaves, with the veined side up, underneath the paper. When they gently rub the crayon over the leaf, a pattern will appear.

When the rubbings are finished, admire the variety of leaves and the patterns they created. You may want to display the leaf rubbings somewhere in the church for others to see.

Next say: Fig trees were highly prized in the Holy Land, providing shade and delicious fruit. The fig tree became a symbol of peace and prosperity to families in Bible times.

Ask kids to bow their heads.

Pray: Dear God, in Bible days, people loved their fig trees. Help us to love our trees too, those beautiful trees that grow by our homes and our schools and our church. Amen.

Serve slices of fresh figs, if you have them, and the fig cookies. Tell kids to pretend they are back in Bible times and that the cookies are really fig cakes. They have been traveling for hours and have just stopped for a snack.

Ask: Don't the fig cakes hit the spot?

Wonder what Eve thought of the fabric of her first dress.

A BIBLE-FOODS TREASURE HUNT
THE TRUE TREASURE

Think about what you truly treasure before setting out on a Bible-Foods Treasure Hunt.

Matthew 13:44

The kingdom of heaven is like treasure hidden in a field, which someone found and hid; then in his joy he goes and sells all that he has and buys that field.

Getting Ready

Food: Small boxes of raisins; honey flavored candy; almonds or candy with almonds; mint-flavored candy

Materials: A treasured item; bags; plastic wrap; Bible

To introduce this activity, you will show kids an item from your own belongings that you treasure.

Make plans to hide the Bible foods for the treasure hunt before the kids arrive. In good weather this is a fine outdoor activity. Make certain you purchase enough of each food so that kids will end up with six or seven items in their bags. Wrap in plastic any foods that aren't already packaged. You may want to set limits on how many items each child may pick up, especially if you have a group of older and younger kids. Older kids tend to be better hunters!

Sampling Treasure

Begin by showing kids the treasure you have brought. Give them details such as where it came from, how long you have had it, and most importantly, why you treasure it. Then ask kids to tell the group about one of their most treasured items.

Say: **We all have things that we treasure. It's fun to have treasures and to think about why they are important to us. But there is a verse in the Bible that tells us that it is even more important to treasure things that we can't hold in our hands.**

Read Matthew 6:19-21.

Ask: **What does it mean to say, "For where your treasure is, there will your heart be also?"** (*What you really cherish or care about will be what is most important to you.*) **What are some treasures that we can't hold in our hands but are treasures that**

God would want us to cherish? (*friendship; love; faith; family ties; talents and abilities*)

Ask kids to fold their hands across their hearts.

Pray: Dear God, we thank you for all the treasure you have given us to hold here on earth. Yet help us to remember that true treasure cannot be held in our hands. Help us to remember that where our treasure is, there will our hearts be also.

Next read Matthew 13:44.

Say: Jesus is comparing God's kingdom to treasure. In the parable a man knew that there was treasure hidden in a field. He sold everything he had to buy the field in order to get that treasure. The treasure was of the utmost importance to him. God wants us to treasure our faith so much that we make it the most important part of our life.

Explain to the kids that to help them remember the parable, they will now be going on a Bible-Foods Treasure Hunt. Tell them to look for foods with raisins, honey, almond, and mint, all foods enjoyed in Bible times.

Treasure in your heart these moments with the children.

When the hunt is finished, kids may eat their treats or save them until later.

A SHEPHERD'S PICNIC
KEEPING WATCH OVER THE FLOCK

Bread, cheese, fruit, and a skit give picnickers a taste of a shepherd's life in Bible times.

John 10:11

I am the good shepherd. The good shepherd lays down his life for the sheep.

Getting Ready

Food: Pita bread; cheese; grapes; raisins, dates, and/or dried figs; grape juice

Materials: Baskets; picnic blankets and cloths; napkins; cups; costumes for two shepherds; photocopies of skits; Bible

Plan to hold this activity outside, with an indoor location in the event of inclement weather.

The skit calls for two players. If your group has two good readers, they can read the skit. Since women took care of sheep too, don't hesitate to make one of the shepherds a shepherdess. If you don't have good readers, recruit teenagers or adults. Make a photocopy of the skit, "The Shepherds' Conversation" for each reader.

Costumes for the shepherds add to the historical flavor. Shawls, table-cloths, sheets, or large pieces of cloth secured with a length of rope or a sash will work well, as will the traditional shepherd's costume, the bathrobe. A simple shepherd's pouch may be made by stuffing a small paper bag with a bit of newspaper. Tie the top of the bag closed and secure the pouch to the shepherd's waist with string. Sandals and a staff will complete the outfit.

Place the foods and the cups and napkins in baskets. Preslicing the cheese and bread eliminates the need for knives.

Sampling a Shepherd's Life

As soon as readers arrive to play the part of the two shepherds, give them their scripts and slip them aside, helping them don their costumes.

When everyone has arrived, bring the shepherds front and center and gather the kids around.

Say: Look! We have visitors today. Shepherds from Bible times! They have invited us to go with them on a Shepherd's Picnic.

Lead the group to the picnic spot, making comments along the way.

For example, say: We need to take care that we don't lose any sheep. Let's hope there aren't any wolves around today. These look like green pastures. Let's stop to let the flock graze here.

When you reach the picnic spot, spread out the blankets and ask everyone to take a seat.

Then say: Now our shepherds are going to have a conversa-tion with one another. Let's listen to what they say. Perhaps we can learn what it was like to be a shepherd in Bible times.

THE SHEPHERDS' CONVERSATION

Shepherd One: Elizabeth told me that she heard of thieves above the hills.

Shepherd Two: Where did you see her?

Shepherd One: At the well. She had quite a time the other day tracking down a lost sheep.

Shepherd Two: She's a good shepherdess. I know it upsets her to lose any sheep.

Shepherd One: You were lucky to get your staff around that lamb yesterday. That was a dangerous climb.

Shepherd Two: It's a good thing we moved to greener pastures today. By the way, did you hear wolves howling last night?

Shepherd One: Yes, and it worries me since it's lambing season.

Shepherd Two: Let's get the flock counted and into the sheepfold early tonight. We have ewes about to give birth.

Shepherd One: Ho! Plenty of fresh milk and cheese soon. The Lord has blessed us.

Shepherd Two: Speaking of food, I'm ready to eat.

Shepherd One: So is your favorite lamb. Here he comes to sniff your pouch.

Shepherd Two: Amazing creatures, sheep. They not only know the sound of the shepherd's voice, but this one knows when it's lunch time!

When the conversation between the shepherds is finished, ask all the other kids to play the part of the sheep and to say "baaaa" in their loudest voices.

Next, read John 10:11, explaining that Jesus is comparing himself to a good shepherd.

Say: Jesus loves and cares for us just as a shepherd cares for sheep.

Let the kids help you spread the picnic cloths, set out the picnic foods, hand out cups and napkins, and pour juice. Explain that this is the sort of food the shepherds in the skit might have had for their lunch.

Pray: God of Yesterday and Today, thank you for this picnic and for your son, Jesus, our Good Shepherd. Amen.

While kids enjoy the picnic, remind them to keep careful watch for wolves.

Here's to you as you watch over your flock!

SAVORING SYMBOLS OF FAITH

PRETZELS
ARMS FOLDED IN PRAYER

The legend of the monk who twisted the first pretzel reminds us of the importance of prayer.

Jude 20

But you, beloved, build yourselves up on your most holy faith; pray in the Holy Spirit.

Getting Ready

Foods: Pretzels (in the traditional shape)

Materials: Bible; bowl or basket

Arrange the pretzels in a bowl or basket.

Practice reading or telling the "Legend of the First Pretzel."

Savoring the Symbol of the Pretzel

Say: There are many verses in the Bible that speak of prayer. Listen to this one from the Book of Jude.

Read Jude 20.

Say: Throughout the Bible we learn how important it is to pray. Prayer is our way of talking to God.

Ask: When you pray, do you fold your hands? (*yes; sometimes*)

Have the kids show you how they fold their hands.

Say: Years ago when people prayed, they folded their arms across

their chests like this. (*Demonstrate how this was done: Fold your arms across your chest, with a hand touching each shoulder.*)

Have kids fold their arms this way.

Next, read or tell the legend of the first pretzel:

LEGEND OF THE FIRST PRETZEL

A long time ago an Italian monk was baking bread in the monastery kitchen. Since it was Lent, he did not put any fat or eggs or sugar into the dough.

While the bread was in the oven, the monk sat down to think and pray. The children in his parish did not seem to be learning their prayers. He was worried because he knew that prayer was important. He wished that he could come up with a clever way to help them. As he thought, he idly rolled a leftover piece of dough between his fingers.

In the Middle Ages children were taught to fold their arms across their chests when they prayed. As he thought and as he rolled the piece of dough, the clever monk suddenly had an idea. He twisted the dough into the outline of praying arms. Then he put it on a pan and baked it, leaving it in the oven perhaps a bit too long. But when he tasted it, he decided it was delicious!

"I will call this treat 'pretiola,' which means 'little reward,'" he said to himself. Perhaps this treat could be a little reward for the children.

That very afternoon the monk baked an entire batch of pretiolas. When the children came to visit, he gave pretiolas to those who knew their prayers.

Before long all the children in the parish began to remember their prayers, and the clever monk baked batch after batch of delicious pretiolas.

After the legend discuss why prayer is important. You may want to emphasize that prayer brings us close to God, that God promises to always hear our prayers, and that there are many types of prayers and ways to pray.

The Lord's Prayer

Our Father, who art in heaven,
   hallowed be thy name,
   Thy kingdom come,
   thy will be done on earth as it
   is in heaven.
Give us this day our daily bread.
And forgive us our trespasses,
   as we forgive those who tres-
   pass against us.
And lead us not into temptation,
   but deliver us from evil.
For thine is the kingdom, and the
   power, and the glory, forever.
Amen.

From The Ritual of the Former Methodist Church, *The United Methodist Hymnal,* © 1989 The United Methodist Publishing House; 895.

When the discussion is finished, ask kids to fold their arms across their chests, as the children did in "The Legend of the First Pretzel." Lead them in a prayer the Italian children might have said, the Lord's Prayer (bottom, previous page).

Invite kids to now enjoy a pretiola, admiring the shape as they do.

Pray as the good monk did, that your kids will understand the importance of prayer.

ANGELS
ICE CREAM CONE CREATIONS

Help orchestrate an Angel Band before enjoying a heavenly treat.

Luke 2:10

But the angel said to them, "Do not be afraid; for see—I am bringing you good news of great joy for all the people."

Getting Ready

Food: Ice cream cones; large marshmallows; ice cream; canned whipping cream; yellow tube frosting

Materials: Bible; spoons; plates; paper doilies; paring knife

For each ice cream cone angel you will need: A sugar cone (with a pointed end), a paper lace doily (heart-shaped or round, about three inches wide), a marshmallow, and a scoop of ice cream. It's best to have extra cones on hand in case some break when you assemble the angels. You will also need canned whipping cream and a tube of yellow frosting.

Partially assemble the angels ahead of time. Place each cone on a small plate. Fold a paper doily in half and reopen. Using the tube frosting, squeeze a dab in the center of the doily. Attach the doily to the cone to make the angel's wings.

With a paring knife make a small slit in the end of a marshmallow. Gently push the marshmallow over the point of the cone. This is the angel's head. To create a halo, squeeze yellow frosting in a circle on top of the marshmallow. Right before serving the angels, create the ice cream base by lifting the angel cone, putting a scoop of ice cream on the plate, squirting a whipped cream cloud around the base, and placing the angel cone on top of the ice cream.

For the angel band you will need metal spoons to serve as rhythm instruments.

Savoring the Symbol of the Angel

Say: Welcome to a celebration of angels! The Bible tells us that angels are God's helpers and messengers. Listen to this story in which angels play an important role.

Read Luke 2:8-20.

Ask: Why are angels important in this story? (*They brought the shepherds the news that Jesus had been born.*)

Say: In the Christmas story, angels sing. In honor of those singing angels, I'm going to turn you into an Angel Band.

Hand each child two metal spoons.

Say: These are angel clappers. Tap them together with gusto as we sing.

Lead the kids in singing "The Angel Choir" (to the tune of "Ten Little Indians").

> ## The Angel Choir
>
> One little, two little, three little angels.
> Four little, five little, six little angels.
> Seven little, eight little, nine little angels.
> Ten little angels in the band!
> Ten little, nine little, eight little angels.
> Seven little, six little, five little angels.
> Four little, three little, two little angels.
> One little angel in the band!

Repeat the song, this time asking kids to march around the room as they sing and clap their spoons. Consider having your Angel Band perform its number for another group or two at church. If your Angel Band is enthusiastic, you may want to lead it in other angel songs such as "Hark! The Herald Angels Sing" or "Angels Watching Over Me."

When the singing is finished, thank the Angel Band.

Say: Now we're going to enjoy an angelic treat in honor of angels.

Scoop ice cream and squirt whipping cream to compete the ice cream cone angels. Before you serve your own little angels, ask them to bow their heads.

Pray: For all the angels, one to ten, Lord of All, we sing "Amen."

congratulations! You earned your angel wings today.

THE CROSS
HOT CROSS BUNS

Honor the most beloved of Christian symbols by marking rolls with the sign of the cross.

Philippians 2:7-8

And being found in human form, he humbled himself and became obedient to the point of death—even death on a cross.

Getting Ready

Food: Canned biscuit dough; tubes of white frosting

Materials: Bible; baking sheets; plates (optional: Mother Goose book)

You may bake the biscuits right before they are to be decorated, or bake them ahead of time and reheat them in the oven or microwave at church. Biscuits may be served cold, if necessary.

If practical, locate a Mother Goose book with an illustration of the rhyme, "Hot Cross Buns," such as Blanche Fisher Wright's *The Real Mother Goose* (Rand McNally, 1916).

Savoring the Symbol of the Cross

Say: The most beloved of Christian symbols is the cross.
Ask: Why is the cross an important symbol of our faith?
(*Because Jesus died on the cross.*)
Read Philippians 2:7-8.
Say: Since Jesus died for us on a cross, we often wear crosses as jewelry or use them to decorate our homes or churches. When we look at the symbol of the cross, we are reminded that Jesus loved us so much that he died for us.
Continue: In ancient times sweet rolls were baked in honor of the Roman goddess of spring, whose name was Eostre. After Jesus died on the cross, the early Christians didn't feel right about eating rolls named in honor of a goddess, since they believed in our God and his son, Jesus Christ. But the rolls were delicious, and they didn't want to give them up! So they began to decorate the rolls with a cross made of white icing.
Continue: In time the rolls were brought by the Romans to England. Soon known as Hot Cross Buns, they were sold by street vendors on Good Friday. Their cry "Hot Cross Buns!" could be heard up and down the streets. This cry inspired a Mother Goose rhyme.

Ask: Does anyone know what that rhyme is? (*Hot Cross Buns*)

If you have an illustration of the rhyme in a Mother Goose book, show it to the kids. Next ask everyone to first recite, then sing, the rhyme with you:

Hot cross buns, hot cross buns,
One a penny, two a penny,
Hot cross buns.

Then say: In honor of the cross we are going to turn ordinary biscuits into our own Hot Cross Buns.

Pass out plates, then the biscuits. Demonstrate how to squeeze the icing in the sign of the cross on top of the biscuit.

When the biscuits have been decorated, admire them before asking kids to bow their heads.

Pray: Dear God, as Christians, we honor Jesus with the symbol of the cross. Bless our Hot Cross Buns. Amen.

one a penny, two a penny, aren't they fun!

CANDY CANES
HONORING THE SHEPHERDS

This traditional Christmas confection reminds us that God cares for us, just as shepherds care for their sheep.

Psalm 23:4

Even though I walk through the darkest valley, I fear no evil; for you are with me; your rod and your staff—they comfort me.

Getting Ready

Food: Candy canes

Materials: Bible; basket (optional: a shepherd's staff or cane)

Place the candy canes in a basket. Keep them out of sight as kids arrive.

Check to see if your church has a shepherd's staff as part of a shepherd's ensemble in your wardrobe collection. If not, perhaps you can locate a cane with a curved handle.

Savoring the Symbol of the Candy Cane

Gather the kids together. Hook the shepherd's staff gently around one of them. Tell the group that you are pretending to be a shepherd using your staff to pull a trapped lamb from a dangerous ledge. (If you haven't been able to locate a staff, you can simply ask kids why they think shepherd's staffs have curved handles.)

Next, give some background on the job of a shepherd in Bible times.

Say: A shepherd is someone who takes care of a flock of sheep. Caring for sheep has never been an easy job, especially in Bible times. Wild animals such as wolves would sometimes try to kill the sheep. To beat off wolves a shepherd carried a heavy stick called a "rod." In order to make sure the flock had enough grass for grazing, the shepherd had to move the sheep to greener pastures. Since the sheep needed to drink too, the shepherd had to lead them to streams. The shepherd's staff was used to prod them along.

Continue: Sometimes a sheep would travel away from the flock and get caught in a crevice or rocky ledge. The crook of the shepherd's staff was used to pull the sheep to safety. The most famous psalm in the Bible, the Twenty-third Psalm, was written by a shepherd. The psalm says God cares for us as a shepherd cares for his sheep.

Read Psalm 24:1-4.

Read the verses again, one line at a time, asking kids to repeat after you.

Ask: How does God care for us as a shepherd cares for sheep? (God helps guide us when we are troubled; God knows when we are sad or worried; even though the world is filled with people, God loves every one of us.)

Say: This psalm is found in the Old Testament. In the New Testament, there is an important story involving shepherds who are out in their fields guarding their flocks by night.

Ask: What story is this? (the Christmas story) What Christmas candy was created in honor of these shepherds? (candy canes)

Say: Legend has it that over one hundred years ago, a candy-maker came up with the idea of forming candy in the shape of a shepherd's staff. We've been enjoying candy canes every since, but not many people know that they were created in honor of the Christmas shepherds.

Bring out the basket of candy canes. Give a candy cane to each child. Next ask the kids to bow their heads.

Pray: Dear God, whenever we eat a candy cane, we will think of your loving staff surrounding us. Thank you for shepherds, thank you for candy canes, and thank you for sending us your son, Jesus. Amen.

If now is a good time for the kids to eat their candy canes, invite them to do so.

When kids are getting ready to leave, explain that you will escort them to the door, one at a time. Crook your arm around the child's shoulder.

Say: Let me shepherd you to the door.

Are there any lost sheep you missed today? Pray for them!

COINS
THE CHEERFUL GIVING GAME

Cookie Coins and the Cheerful Giving Game help us focus on giving as we count our own blessings.

Luke 21:3

He said, "Truly I tell you, this poor widow has put in more than all of them."

Getting Ready

Foods: Round sandwich cookies

Materials: Bible; aluminum foil; box for cookie coins; photocopies of the Cheerful Giving Game (optional: envelopes and crayons)

To create cookie coins, wrap sandwich cookies in aluminum foil, two or three per child. Place them in an attractive box with a lid.

Make copies of the Cheerful Giving Game, one per child. This activity encourages kids to collect coins for a mission project. Decide where the money you collect will be donated.

You may want to have the kids decorate envelopes to hold the coins they collect.

The Cheerful Giving Game

Each day of the week, put the correct amount of change into an envelope.

SUNDAY: Five cents for every pair of shoes in your closet.

MONDAY: Ten cents for every time you talk to a friend on the phone.

TUESDAY: Twenty-five cents if you eat any candy.

WEDNESDAY: One cent for every electrical appliance in your house.

THURSDAY: Fifteen cents if you listen to music.

FRIDAY: Twenty-five cents if you have ice cream, soda, or pizza.

SATURDAY: Ten cents for every TV show you watch.

SAVORING THE SYMBOL OF THE COIN

Say: **I'm going to read a Bible story called "The Widow's Offering."**

Read the story (also known as "The Widow's Mite") from Luke 21:1-4.

Ask: **Even though rich people put in lots of money, why did Jesus say that the widow had put in more than all of them?** (*Because she put in all the money she had to live on.*)

Say: **As Christians we are called to share what we have. This week you are going to play the Cheerful Giving Game. The game is named after a verse in the Bible that says, "God loves a cheerful giver"** (*2 Corinthians 9:7*).

Explain where the money the kids collect will be donated. Hand out copies of the game and answer any questions. Have the kids decorate envelopes, perhaps with smiling faces, if you have decided to do this.

Next, bring out the coin box and shake it a few times.

Say: **In the story of the widow the two copper coins are a symbol of her generosity. When you play the Cheerful Giving Game at home, your coins will be a symbol of your generosity too.**

Shake the box again.

Ask: **Can you guess what's inside the box?**

After the kids have guessed, open the box and pass out the cookie coins.

Say: **While we aren't supposed to eat real coins, these are cookie coins, and they taste delicious.**

Before the kids unwrap and eat their coins, have them bow their heads.

Pray: **Dear God, just like the widow in the story, help us to share what we have. And when we give, may we do so with a smile, because we know that you love cheerful givers! Amen.**

A penny for your thoughts.

In the next few weeks you may need to remind kids to return the coins they collected in the Cheerful Giving Game.

BOATS
THE CHURCH AND HER BELIEVERS

Pay tribute to this early symbol of the church and its believers by taking a pretend boat ride, then building Believer Boats out of pear halves and miniature marshmallows.

Mark 4:39

He woke up and rebuked the wind, and said to the sea, "Peace! Be still!" Then the wind ceased, and there was a dead calm.

Getting Ready

Foods: Canned pear halves; miniature marshmallows

Materials: Bible; two serving bowls; bowls or plates; forks; masking tape (optional: spray water bottle)

Drain the pear halves and place them in a serving bowl. Put the marshmallows in another bowl.

Use masking tape to mark off the shape of a simple boat on the floor. (You may need to find a larger space in the church to do this.) You and the kids will sit in the boat and pretend you are caught in a storm. Make certain the boat is big enough to seat everyone comfortably.

Savoring the Symbol of the Boat

Lead the kids to the boat, bringing your Bible with you.

Say: **We're going to take a boat ride today. Step in carefully and sit down. We don't want to rock the boat because we don't want anyone to fall overboard!**

Let the kids get settled.

Say: **My, the weather looks like it's getting bad. I hope the water doesn't become rough.** (*Begin to rock back and forth.*) **Oh my! This is getting choppy.** (*Encourage the kids to rock back and forth too. If you have brought a spray bottle, spray the kids a time or two.*) **I am really scared!**

Continue for a minute or so.

Say: **Oh good! It looks like the sky is clearing. The waters are calming.** (*Begin rocking less and less until you stop completely.*) **My, that was scary.**

Ask: **Why would it be scary to be riding in a boat in a bad storm?** (*You might be thrown overboard; the boat might sink; you might become sick.*)

110

Say: There is a story in the Bible about Jesus and a scary storm at sea.

Read Mark 4:35-41.

Ask: What does this story tell us about Jesus? (*He could perform miracles; he can help us when we are afraid.*)

Say: Early in the history of the Christian church, the ship or boat became a symbol of the church and her believers. The passengers on the boat are the believers, the people worshiping inside the church. In many church buildings the central section, where the people sit, is called the "nave." This word comes from the Latin word for "ship." Our word *navy* also comes from this Latin word. Now it's time to go ashore and create a snack. In honor of the symbol of the boat, we're going to make Believer Boats.

After kids disembark from the pretend boat, lead them to prepare the snack. Serve each child a pear half. Explain that the marshmallows are to be the believers and they are to be placed in the pear boat, turning the pear into a Believer Boat.

Row, row, row . . .

Pray: God of Land and God of Sea, we're glad that we are passengers on the boat of the Christian church, sailing away with our fellow believers. Amen.

EGGS
REMEMBERING THE RESURRECTION

Encounter this ancient symbol of the Resurrection, then concoct your very own Angelic Deviled Eggs.

1 Peter 1:3

Blessed be the God and Father of our Lord Jesus Christ! By his great mercy he has given us a new birth into a living hope through the resurrection of Jesus Christ from the dead.

Getting Ready

Food: Eggs (hardboiled); mayonnaise; salt; pepper; paprika; candy eggs or jellybeans

Materials: Mixing bowl; measuring spoons or tablespoons; knives; spoons; forks; paper towels; Bible

You will need one hardboiled egg per child, and a few extras.

Kids will enjoy a treat of a candy egg too. In the spring you can find many sorts of candy eggs, but jelly beans are available year round.

Savoring the Symbol of the Egg

Gather the kids together. Begin by holding up a hardboiled egg.

Ask: What's this? (*an egg*) May I have a volunteer? I want to crack this egg over someone's head. (*If you can't coax a volunteer, crack the egg over your own head.*)

Say: Thank goodness this is a hardboiled egg. Otherwise, what a mess!

Say: Raise your hand if you like the following kinds of eggs: (*List the types of eggs one at a time*): scrambled, hard-boiled, deviled, omelets, fried.

Then ask: What about marshmallow eggs? Jelly beans? Chocolate eggs?

Continue: What time of year do we decorate eggs and enjoy candy eggs? (*Easter*) For many centuries, the egg has been a symbol of Easter.

Ask: What comes out of eggs that have been fertilized? (*chicks; birds; snakes; crocodiles*)

Say: Since live animals emerge from eggs, eggs represent new life.

Ask: On Easter Sunday who came out of the tomb? (*Jesus*)

Say: Just as an animal comes out of an egg, Jesus, who was dead, came out of the tomb alive. In time, Christians began to associate the new life that emerges from an egg with Jesus, who emerged from a tomb. This is how eggs became a symbol of the Resurrection.

Read 1 Peter 1:3, telling kids that this is one of many verses in the Bible that refers to the joyful news of the Resurrection of Jesus.

Say: Today, in celebration of the symbol of the egg, you are going to become chefs and prepare Deviled Eggs. In cooking terms to "devil" means to "chop a food into fine pieces and then to season." But we are going to call our eggs "Angelic Deviled Eggs" to make them sound even more heavenly delicious.

Give each child a paper towel, a knife, a spoon, a fork, and an egg. Show the kids how to crack the egg in two, peel off the shell, slice the egg in half, and scoop out the yolk with a spoon into the mixing bowl. If there are extra eggs, put those in too.

Add about a tablespoon of mayonnaise for every two eggs. The kids can help with this, then take turns mashing the yokes into the mayonnaise with forks, and then adding salt and pepper. Next, have them spoon the mixed yoke back into their egg halves and decorate each with a sprinkling of paprika.

Praise the chefs, then say a prayer before kids eat the Angelic Deviled Eggs.

Pray: Father of the Risen Jesus, when we eat eggs, we will try to remember that they are a symbol of Easter and the new life of the Resurrection. Amen.

And thanks for being such a good egg!

As kids are eating their deviled eggs, hand out the candy eggs, if you have brought them.

TRIANGLES
CHEESY TRINITY TRIANGLES

Learn more about the significance of the Trinity before enjoying Cheesy Trinity Triangles.

2 Corinthians 13:13

The grace of the Lord Jesus Christ, the love of God, and the communion of the Holy Spirit be with all of you.

Getting Ready

Foods: Sliced bread; cheese slices

Materials: Baking sheets; spatula; plates; Bible

You may want to slice the bread and the cheese into triangle halves ahead of time. Cheesy Trinity Triangles are best baked in a hot oven until the cheese melts. If you are going to need to cook them in a microwave, toast the bread ahead of time.

Savoring the Symbol of the Trinity

Gather the kids together.

Say: Today I'm going to teach you to do the Trinity Stretch.
Ask kids to stand, then lead them in several rounds of the stretch:

In the name of the Father, (*Cross arms across chest.*)
In the name of the Son, (*Hold arms straight out from the sides so that the body forms a cross.*)
And in the name of the Holy Spirit. (*Hold arms straight above head, then wiggle fingers as arms are moved slowly down.*)

You may want to explain that the crossed arms represent God as a loving Father; the arms out straight represent Jesus, since they form a cross with the body; and the wiggling fingers represent a dove, the symbol of the Holy Spirit.

Ask kids to sit back down.

Say: Today we are celebrating the Trinity. In the Christian church we believe in one God, but we know God as three different persons: God the Father, God the Son, who is Jesus, and God the Holy Spirit, who is the spirit of God living among us. The word *trinity* comes from the Latin word *tri*, which means "triple" or "three."

Ask: Can you think of the name of a shape that comes from this Latin word too? (*triangle*)

Say: For Christians the triangle has become a symbol of the Trinity.

Ask: Can anyone guess why? (*Because the triangle has three sides and three points.*)

Say: When you see a triangle, remember that one side or point can represent God the Father, another side or point can represent Jesus, God's son, and another side or point can represent the Holy Spirit. All of the sides and points together make one triangle, just as the three persons in the Trinity together are one God.

Read 2 Corinthians 13:13, asking kids to listen for the names of all three persons of the Trinity.

Announce that the time has come to celebrate the symbol of the triangle by making Cheesy Trinity Triangles. Have the kids put the bread triangles on cookie sheets and top each with a triangle cheese slice.

While the triangles are cooking (it only takes a few minutes for the cheese to melt), lead the group in singing

Glory Be to the Father

**Glory be to the Father
and to the Son and to the Holy Ghost;
as it was in the beginning,
is now, and ever shall be,
world without end. Amen. Amen.**

Lesser Doxology, 3rd—4th cent.

Use the spatula to put the Cheesy Trinity Triangles on plates, then serve.

May God the Father, God the Son, and God the Holy Spirit uphold you as you work with children.

BUTTERFLIES
CREATIONS of NEW LIFE

Talk about this symbol of new life, then create Butterfly Crackers and colorful butterfly magnets.

2 Corinthians 5:17

So if anyone is in Christ, there is a new creation: everything old has passed away; see, everything has become new!

Getting Ready

Foods: Oval and snack stick crackers (rod shaped); canned squirt cheese

Materials: Plates; 3-by-5-inch index cards; magnetic strips with adhesive backing; paints; brushes; glue; construction paper; Bible (optional: a book with photographs or illustrations of butterflies)

To create Butterfly Crackers, kids will place two oval crackers touching side by side, squirt a stripe of cheese where the crackers meet, and place a rod-shaped cracker in the center.

Along with a book that shows the amazing variety of butterflies in nature, consider locating Eric Carle's picture book, *The Very Hungry Caterpillar* (Putnam, 1984), the story of a caterpillar who becomes a beautiful butterfly.

Kids will make two butterfly magnets, one to decorate the refrigerator at church and one for their refrigerator at home. Butterflies will be made with a magnetic strip body about two or three inches long, index card wings, and a construction paper strip to cover the body. Wings will be formed by folding index cards in half horizontally and snipping. Construction paper slips should be about the size of the magnetic strip. The wings will be placed over the adhesive side of the magnetic stripping and the construction paper body placed over them. For younger kids you may want to precut the materials.

Kids will decorate the wings by putting dabs of paint on one side, then rubbing the sides together to create a pattern on both sides. Acrylic paints will give more vibrant colors, but watercolors will work too. Only a few dabs of paint in several colors are needed.

Savoring the Symbol of the Butterfly

Begin by holding up a picture of a butterfly from the book.

Ask: What's this? (*a butterfly*)

Show kids more illustrations of butterflies, allowing them to make comments on the many varieties. (If you haven't been able to locate a butterfly book, you can ask kids to describe the butterflies they have seen.)

Ask: Do butterflies always look like this? (*No, they begin life as a caterpillar.*)

Explain that caterpillars spin themselves into a chrysalis or cocoon, emerging after a period of time as a butterfly. (Read *The Very Hungry Caterpillar,* if you have it.)

Then say: The caterpillar changes into a butterfly. For Christians the butterfly has become a symbol of new life, the life we have through our faith in Jesus.

Read 2 Corinthians 5:17.

Ask: What does it mean to have new life in Jesus? (*While we live on earth, Jesus guides and enriches our lives; when we die, we will have a new life in heaven.*)

Say: Remember, when you see a caterpillar or a butterfly, to stop and think about the new life that Christians have through their faith in Jesus.

Demonstrate how to make the butterfly magnets, explaining that kids will make one to decorate the refrigerator at church and one for their refrigerators at home.

When the magnets are finished, show kids how to construct Butterfly Crackers.

Before they eat their snack, ask them to stand, put their hands on their hips to resemble butterfly wings, and bow their heads.

Pray: Dear God, we thank you for butterflies, and we thank you for Jesus, who promises new life for all who believe in him. Amen.

After the snack ask kids to follow you to the church kitchen, bringing one of their butterfly magnets. When the magnets are arranged on the refrigerator, admire them! When you return, remind kids that the other magnets are to decorate their refrigerators at home with the symbol of the butterfly.

The next time you see a butterfly flutter by, thank God for new life.

STARS
A STARRY CELEBRATION

Take part in a Starry Celebration complete with a Star Search, a starry song and poem, a Starry Skies Poster, and a starry apple snack.

Matthew 2:2

Where is the child who has been born king of the Jews? For we observed his star at its rising, and have come to pay him homage.

Getting Ready

Foods: Apples; peanut butter; cinnamon sugar

Materials: Bible; sharp knife; plates; construction paper; scissors; ball of yarn; stapler; dark colored poster board; glitter, glue; gummed stars (optional: recording of "We Three Kings" and player)

For the snack you will slice an apple in half to show kids the star, then slice apples to create Apple Stars. Kids will spread peanut butter and sprinkle cinnamon sugar on their Apple Stars. A medium-sized apple should yield about five slices.

The activity will begin with a Star Hunt. Kids will follow a length of yarn marked with paper stars. At the end of the yarn they will discover supplies for making the Starry Skies Poster. Cut out simple construction paper stars to be placed every several feet along the length of yarn. Before the activity, unroll yarn from the starting point to the location where you will place the craft supplies. Attach stars to the yarn with a stapler. Depending on the layout of your church or churchyard, you may want to have the Star Hunt take the kids on a roundabout route to the craft supplies. At the end of the yarn set out the craft supplies of glitter, glue, gummed stars, and posterboard.

Savoring the Symbol of the Star

Begin by reading the story of the wise men (Matthew 2:1-12).

Then ask: Why is a star important in this story? (*The star led the wise men to baby Jesus.*)

Say: Since the star led the wise men to baby Jesus, the star has become a symbol of the birth of Jesus and the light that Jesus brings into the world.

If you have located a recording of "We Three Kings," play the song for the kids to hear. If not, hum the melody, asking them to identify it. Then lead them in singing the first verse:

We three kings of Orient are; bearing gifts we traverse afar, field and fountain, moor and mountain, following yonder star. O star of wonder, star of light, star with royal beauty bright, westward leading, still proceeding, guide us to thy perfect light.

John H. Hopkins, Jr., 1857 (Matthew 2:1-12).

You may also want to sing that old favorite, "Twinkle, Twinkle Little Star."

Next, ask the kids to bow their heads.

Pray: Dear God, we thank you for the star that guided the wise men, for the stars that twinkle in our sky at night, and most of all for sending the light of Jesus into the world. Amen.

Next, send kids on the Star Hunt, encouraging them to think about the wise men as they follow the paper stars. Explain that they will find the next activity at the end of the string of stars and that they should bring the supplies back with them.

Have the kids create the Starry Skies Poster by filling the dark sky of the posterboard with stars and glitter. When the poster is finished, admire it and let the kids help decide where to hang it.

Next, announce that the time has come for a starry snack. Show kids the star in the apple by slicing an apple in half horizontally. As you do, say this poem: "When we slice the apple and see the star, we remember the wise men, who came from afar." Ask kids to say it with you a few times as you slice Apple Stars for everyone. Invite them to spread peanut butter on some stars and sprinkle cinnamon on others. Of course, they may try a combination of the two, if they like!

Tonight, step outside and make a wish upon a star.